ALASKA GEOGRAPHIC

Volume 19, Number 4

Alaska's Railroads

The Alaska Geographic Society

To teach many more to better know and more wisely use our natural resources

EDITOR
Penny Rennick

PRODUCTION DIRECTOR
Kathy Doogan

STAFF WRITER
L.J. Campbell

MARKETING MANAGER
Jan Westfall

BUSINESS & CIRCULATION MANAGER
Kevin Kerns

POSTMASTER: Send address changes to
ALASKA GEOGRAPHIC®
P.O. Box 93370
Anchorage, Alaska 99509-3370

PRICE TO NON-MEMBERS THIS ISSUE: $18.95

COVER:
The Alaska Railroad, flagship of the state's rail lines, passes through the Alaska Range near Denali National Park. (John W. Warden)

PREVIOUS PAGE:
British money, American engineering and Canadian contracting combined to build the oldest of Alaska's currently operating railroads, the White Pass and Yukon, shown here at its operational headquarters at Skagway. (Danny Daniels)

FACING PAGE:
The Alaska Railroad winds through Nenana Canyon, along the Nenana River north of Denali National Park. (Charles Kay)

ALASKA GEOGRAPHIC® (ISSN 0361-1353) is published quarterly by The Alaska Geographic Society, 639 W International, Unit 38, Anchorage, AK 99518. Second-class postage paid at Anchorage, Alaska, and additional mailing offices. Printed in U.S.A. Copyright © 1992 by The Alaska Geographic Society. All rights reserved. Registered trademark: Alaska Geographic, ISSN 0361-1353; Key title Alaska Geographic.

THE ALASKA GEOGRAPHIC SOCIETY is a non-profit organization exploring new frontiers of knowledge across the lands of the Polar Rim, putting the geography book back in the classroom, exploring new methods of teaching and learning—sharing in the excitement of discovery in man's wonderful new world north of 51°16'.

SOCIETY MEMBERS receive *ALASKA GEOGRAPHIC®*, a quality magazine that devotes each quarterly issue to monographic in-depth coverage of a northern geographic region or resource-oriented subject.

MEMBERSHIP in The Alaska Geographic Society costs $39 per year, $49 to non-U.S. addresses. ($31.20 of the $39 is for a one-year subscription to *ALASKA GEOGRAPHIC®*.) Order from The Alaska Geographic Society, P.O. Box 93370, Anchorage, AK 99509-3370; phone (907) 562-0164, FAX (907) 562-0479.

SUBMITTING PHOTOGRAPHS: Please write for a list of upcoming topics or other specific photo needs and a copy of our editorial guidelines. We cannot be responsible for unsolicited submissions. Submissions not accompanied by sufficient postage for return by certified mail will be returned by regular mail.

CHANGE OF ADDRESS: The post office does not automatically forward *ALASKA GEOGRAPHIC®* when you move. To ensure continuous service, please notify us six weeks before moving. Send your new address, and, if possible, your membership number or a mailing label from a recent *ALASKA GEOGRAPHIC®* to: The Alaska Geographic Society, P.O. Box 93370, Anchorage, AK 99509-3370.

MAILING LISTS: We occasionally make our members' names and addresses available to carefully screened publications and companies whose products and activities may be of interest to you. If you prefer not to receive such mailings, please advise us, and include your mailing label (or your name and address if label is not available).

COLOR SEPARATIONS BY: Graphic Chromatics

PRINTED BY: Hart Press

ISBN: 1-56661-006-0 (paper);
1-56661-007-9 (hardback)

ABOUT THIS ISSUE: Railroads have played an important role in the development of Alaska, so the *ALASKA GEOGRAPHIC®* staff thought it was time to take a closer look at some of the major iron roads that brought supplies to the pioneers, took out the gold, copper and other natural resources and continue to serve the state's economy.

Award-winning author Roy Minter wrote the chapter on the White Pass and Yukon Railway, his employer for many years. Lone Janson, whose family members worked on the line, contributed the article on the Copper River & Northwestern Railroad and the challenges of construction near Alaska's glaciers. Editor Penny Rennick wrote a piece on the various railroad ventures that sought to exploit the gold of the Seward Peninsula, and Fairbanks resident Debbie S. Miller acquaints readers with the pioneering efforts of Falcon Joslin and his Tanana Valley Railroad. In "Dynamite and Gandy Dancers," staff writer L.J. Campbell recounts the history of the flagship of the state's rail lines, the Alaska Railroad, and free-lance writer Jeffrey R. Richardson tells readers about a female gandy dancer crew in "I Worked to Survive." For an overview of the economic impact of railroads on the state and a discussion of schemes to expand the lines, the staff turned to Rose Ragsdale, former business editor for the *Anchorage Times* and now a business and economics writer. Finally, we thank Bill Sherwonit, free-lance writer and former outdoors columnist for the *Anchorage Times* for his piece on the Grandview Ski Train, a winter ritual for Anchorage Nordic skiers.

We appreciate the research assistance of Mina Jacobs and Diane Brenner at the Anchorage Museum, and of Bruce Merrell and Dan Fleming of the Loussac Library's Alaska Collection in Anchorage. We thank Dick Knapp of the Alaska Railroad for reviewing portions of the manuscript, and appreciate the personal reminiscences of Tim McKeown and Virgie Hartley-McKeown, whose relative John R. Van Cleve worked on several of Alaska's railroads in the early days.

The Library of Congress has cataloged this serial publication as follows:

Alaska Geographic. v.1-
    [Anchorage, Alaska Geographic Society] 1972-
    v. ill. (part col.). 23 x 31 cm.
    Quarterly
    Official publication of The Alaska Geographic Society.
    Key title: Alaska geographic, ISSN 0361-1353.

    1. Alaska—Description and travel—1959-
    —Periodicals. I. Alaska Geographic Society.

F901.A266   917.98'04'505   72-92087

Library of Congress   75[79112]   MARC-S

Contents

The White Pass:
Gateway to the Yukon

By Roy Minter

Editor's note: *Roy Minter was born in London, but moved to Vancouver, British Columbia, at an early age. A career Canadian Army officer, he was last assigned to Headquarters, Northwest Highway System, Whitehorse, Yukon, in 1955. He retired from the Army in 1957 and joined the White Pass and Yukon Corp. as Special Assistant to the President. Subsequently he was appointed a vice president of the corporation, a position he held until he retired in 1973. Mr. Minter's award-winning book,* The White Pass - Gateway to the Klondike *was published in 1987. He has long been active in promotion of tourism in the Yukon. In 1986 he was presented with the Commissioner's Award for service to the Yukon; in 1988 he received the Yukon Heritage Award and in April 1991 he was appointed to the Order of Canada.*

On July 29, 1900, they drove home the last spike on the White Pass and Yukon Railway at Carcross, Yukon, an event that linked the Yukon with ocean traffic and created one of the most spectacular railway rides in the world.

Today, 92 years later, thousands of summertime passengers climb aboard the train that parallels the Trail of '98 where, it is said, ghosts of Klondike days still linger among the massive shoulders of granite that shape the White Pass from Skagway, Alaska, to its historic summit 20 miles to the north.

Riverboat captain William Moore was the first person to visualize the need for a railway through White Pass. Ten years before the rush to the Klondike he predicted that one day gold would be discovered in the Yukon, and that a railway would be required to support the diggings.

William Ogilvie, leader of a Canadian Yukon River survey, facetiously reported to Ottawa in 1887 that Moore, who was a member of his party, was convinced "the White Pass would reverberate with the rumble of railway trains carrying supplies, and its peaks and valleys would echo and re-echo to their signal whistles."

FACING PAGE:
Diesel engines pull the train through one of two tunnels on the spectacular climb from sea level at Skagway to the White Pass summit. At mile 16 the line crosses Glacier Gorge and enters Tunnel Mountain, dug out during the original construction of the line at the end of the 1800s. The second tunnel was built in the late 1960s. (Stephen Rasmussen)

Nobody believed Moore's prophesy, but he was so convinced that one day there would be a major gold rush to the Yukon he left Ogilvie's survey and, with his son Ben, staked 160 acres of land at the tip of Lynn Canal, an inspired decision that made him the founder of Skagway.

Moore and his son worked for years without success trying to convince private investors as well as governments in Canada and the United States that there would be need of a trail, and a road, and eventually a railroad through White Pass to support his prophesied gold rush. At every turn both he and his project were understandably rejected out of hand.

This was the situation when in January 1896 Charles Herbert Wilkinson, an English engineer acting for the British Columbia Development Association Ltd. arrived in Victoria, British Columbia, from London, seeking investment opportunities.

Shortly after his arrival he met Captain Moore who, at 74, was still vigorous and optimistic. Wilkinson soon fell under old Moore's spell and, after an extensive and personal review of Moore's claims, he recommended to his London syndicate that, because of developments all along the Yukon River in both Alaska and the Yukon, they undertake to build a railway from Skagway to the Yukon border.

London subsequently informed Wilkinson that his railway recommendation was accepted, and that he was to incorporate the necessary companies, and obtain the required rights and charters from the governments of Canada and the United States.

The immediate problem Wilkinson faced was the unresolved question of which nation controlled the Alaska Panhandle. This meant incorporating a railway that would cross territory claimed by both Canada and the United States. He decided that this could best be achieved by forming three companies, one American and two Canadian.

On November 14, 1896, he incorporated the Pacific & Arctic Railway & Navigation Co. under the laws of West Virginia. Its main objective was to construct a railway from Skagway Bay to the international border that, when established, would define the line of demarcation between Alaska and British Columbia.

His second company, the British Columbia-Yukon Railway, was incorporated in Victoria, under the laws of British Columbia on April 22, 1897. It was authorized to construct a railway from a point on, or near, Lynn Canal to the border between British Columbia and the Yukon. Should the politicians subsequently declare Skagway a Canadian port, the company would be able to build from Skagway clear to the British Columbia-Yukon border, eliminating the need of the Pacific & Arctic Railway & Navigation Co.

The third company, the British Yukon Mining, Trading and Transportation Co., was incorporated in Ottawa on June 29, 1897. It was authorized to "construct and operate a railway...from a point in British Columbia...near the head of Lynn Canal, thence across the White Pass to Fort Selkirk," which was the original destination of the railway, but later abandoned.

By these clever moves Wilkinson erected a corporate edifice, known collectively as The White Pass and Yukon Railway, which was capable of accommodating itself to any Panhandle border subsequently established by the politicians of Canada, the United States and Great Britain.

His timing could not have been better for on July 17, 1897, the steamer *Portland*'s arrival in Seattle set the West Coast aflame with its ton of gold and news of the discovery of gold in the Klondike.

Steve Hites, a Skagway businessmen, is conductor on this White Pass run as it leaves Carcross, Yukon Territory, on the shores of Lake Bennett. In the background is the sternwheeler, Tutshi. *During construction of the railroad, crews coming from Whitehorse and those coming from Skagway met at Carcross on July 29, 1900. (Danny Daniels)*

John R. Van Cleve (right) shares the shop office of the White Pass and Yukon with Tom Standick, Agnes McCaughey and three unidentified workers. John R. Van Cleve worked on three of Alaska's pioneering railroads, the White Pass, Copper River & Northwestern and Alaska Railroad. He married Clara Goding in Kalispell, Mont., in 1898, and came directly to Alaska, arriving in 1899. The couple had three children: Charlotte, born in Sitka in 1900; Margaret, born in Sitka in 1903; and John R., born in Cordova in 1905. (Case and Draper Photo; from the Van Cleve Family, courtesy of Tim and Virgie McKeown)

It was at this point that disaster struck. The syndicate ran out of money. As a result, Wilkinson and his associates were forced to relinquish the entire railway project to their principal creditor, a major British financial house known as Close Brothers of London.

Close Brothers' reaction was immediate. Gold rush activity was boiling on the West Coast of North America and, despite restrictions imposed by the Spanish-American War, Senior Partner William Brooks Close dispatched railway expert Sir Thomas Tancred to Skagway with Erastus Corning Hawkins, an American engineer, and John Hislop, a Canadian surveyor. Their instructions were to determine the feasibility of building a railway through White Pass from tidewater to the interior of the Yukon.

After examining both sides of the pass, Sir Thomas doubted the viability of the project, an opinion rejected by both Hawkins and Hislop.

A chance meeting in a Skagway hotel bar, however, with Canadian railway contractor Michael James Heney resolved the issue. Heney, who had just completed an independent survey of the pass, was convinced that the railway could be built, and that he was the man to build it.

After an all-night discussion in Skagway's St. James Hotel, Sir Thomas finally agreed.

Sir Thomas, with Close Brothers' approval, offered Heney a position as general foreman of construction. Hawkins would be in charge as chief engineer and general manager with Hislop acting as his assistant.

The first break came for Close Brothers on May 14, 1898, when Congress extended provisions of the United States land laws to Alaska. This permitted Samuel H. Graves, Close Brothers' representative in North America and the railway's

In July 1898, the first White Pass locomotive chugged four miles up the tracks; two years later all the track was laid. But even before the track was completely finished, passengers rode the White Pass to the summit for a day's outing from Skagway. (Anchorage Museum, Photo No. B64.1.73)

first president, to obtain a right-of-way from Skagway to White Pass summit despite the fact that the Panhandle question had yet to be settled.

Graves wasted no time. By May 28, 1898, just two weeks after Congress had extended the land laws to Alaska, the first loads of railway construction material landed on the beaches of Skagway, and by the first week of June construction crews were slashing their way north through the coastal forest.

Only six weeks later the railway's first locomotive was fired up and sent puffing four miles up the pass.

Day in and day out Hawkins and Heney and their construction gangs attacked the gigantic saddles of glacier-scarred rock, creating as they went a 14-foot right-of-way with a grade that never exceeded 4 percent. Month after month in the hazy heat of summer and blue cold of winter they blasted, filled, graded and tunneled their way to the summit. Men hung from ropes to chip footholds in the perpendicular massifs so they could drill the blast holes for the dynamite and black powder. A reporter for the old *Alaska Magazine* wrote: "It was a strange sight to see the workmen hanging from a stout line half way up the precipitous mountainside, where there was scarcely footing for an eagle."

With nothing but horses, black powder, picks, shovels and men, they blasted and hacked their way north to the summit and beyond to Lake Bennett, terminal point of the first section.

The second section from Bennett north was built by Heney who, acting as an independent contractor, obtained a subcontract to complete the

last 70 miles of railway to Whitehorse, Yukon Territory. Hawkins, however, remained in charge of the project.

Heavy rock work along Lake Bennett consumed hundreds of tons of explosives, and the work beyond Carcross was plagued with permafrost, quagmires and the ever-present problem of replacing men who abandoned the work force whenever rumors hit the construction camps about another gold strike in the surrounding hills.

After 26 months of blasting, grading and laying rail, the first locomotive reached Whitehorse on June 8, 1900, though travel by boats was required to bridge the gap in rails along Lake Bennett. The last spike was driven at Carcross on July 29, an event that was witnessed by a boisterous crowd from Skagway and Whitehorse who had arrived fully equipped

FACING PAGE:
Engineer Fred Brayford brings No. 56 into the summit of White Pass. (H. Barley Photo; from the Van Cleve Family, courtesy of Tim and Virgie McKeown)

LEFT:
A major challenge to builders of the White Pass and Yukon was the chasm near the upper end of Dead Horse Gulch. Contractor Michael J. Heney originally laid a switch-back to get the trains around this obstacle. Later a permanent steel arch cantilever bridge was constructed, spanning the gorge 215 feet above its floor. (Anchorage Museum, Photo No. B88.3.42)

with bottles of hospitality and a hearty thirst.

Thus we see the completion of the White Pass line by Hawkins, Heney, Hislop and Graves, a railway constructed by British money, American engineering and Canadian contracting.

To this day, Skagway remains its operational headquarters. From there trains are dispatched, rolling stock maintained, repairs completed.

For 82 years the railway was the Yukon's major overland transportation corridor and during that time, it never stopped hauling freight and passengers in and out of the Yukon. Business, however, was minimal throughout the 1920s and the depression years of the 1930s.

For years prior to World War II, red ink was the predominant color in its books. At one point, the railway's president, Herbert Wheeler, mortgaged his house to meet the payroll.

The White Pass lived through World War I and was so important to the war effort during World

In this photo taken in 1975 passengers look through a window to the diesel engines rounding a curve ahead. Contemporary White Pass passenger cars have stationary seats, oil stoves and modern plumbing, but passengers in earlier times traveled in cars with pot-bellied stoves, moveable seats and plumbing that emptied onto the tracks. (Harry M. Walker)

War II that the whole railway was leased and operated by the U.S. Army and used as a major supply route for construction of the Alaska Highway.

The post-war years were vigorous. A renewed gloss appeared on the Yukon's golden crown. Mines were opening, tourism was up, and the Yukon was making marked advances in its political development.

Then came 1982.

That was the year the railway reeled under a near-fatal blow. It had spent millions of dollars upgrading its system to accommodate the Yukon's robust mining industry. Then suddenly, due to low world metal prices and the 1982 recession, every mine in the Yukon closed down for an extended period of time. Although the industry has recovered, the closures threw northbound freight tonnage into a free fall. Under these circumstances the railway, in early October 1982, had no alternative but to suspend operations.

This was the first shutdown in its history, a traumatic experience for a railway that had participated in every major development in Skagway, the Yukon and northern British Columbia since the discovery of gold in the Klondike.

The suspension rocked railway fans throughout

FAR LEFT:
Brakeman and conductor John Jackson poses outside one of the passenger cars on the White Pass and Yukon. (Harry M. Walker)

ABOVE:
Engineer D.J. True checks the train from his position in Engine No. 73 of the White Pass and Yukon line. Steam engines pull the train out of Skagway for a short distance, then diesels are connected to power the train up the steep route to the summit at mile 20.4. (Danny Daniels)

the world. The demand for its services as a tourist attraction were persistent. After examining the market, Marvin Taylor, the railway's president, reinstated tourist passenger service from Skagway to White Pass summit in 1988, the most scenic, dramatic and historic portion of the line.

With barely no promotion or advertising, the railway carried nearly 40,000 passengers in 1988, 77,000 in 1989, nearly 90,000 in 1990 and more than 101,000 in 1991. Taylor states that there is every indication that 1992 will exceed 1991's total by 10 percent.

The company has also inaugurated a passenger motor car operation between Fraser, British Columbia, and Bennett, British Columbia, to accommodate Chilkoot Trail hikers, and the U.S. National Park Service and Parks Canada. In 1991 nearly 2,000 hikers used this special service.

During the year 2000, the railway will celebrate its 100th anniversary, and there is every reason to think that White Pass diesel locomotives will still be hauling passenger trains through the White Pass where the old Trail of '98 is still plain to see, right beside the track.

Snoose, Overalls, Whiskey and Snowballs:
Building the Copper River & Northwestern Railroad

By Lone Janson

Editor's note: *The author of* The Copper Spike *(1975), Lone Janson came to Alaska in 1945 looking for adventure. She now lives in Anchorage where she continues her writing projects.*

Michael J. Heney, builder of two of the three major railroads in Alaska, had a philosophy: "Give me enough dynamite and whiskey, and I'll build you a road to Hell!" He was a man of action, and there was plenty of action in Alaska in the early 1900s. The gold rush was still on, and in the Wrangell Mountains the Kennecott Mine Co.'s Bonanza Mine held one of the richest copper ore deposits ever discovered. The Guggenheim-Morgan Syndicate lost no time in acquiring it, and began construction of a railroad from Valdez in 1905. Other railroad lines were also competing.

Heney, fresh from his triumph in building the White Pass and Yukon Railway out of Skagway, watched the action carefully, for he had learned that the Guggenheim engineers had investigated a route up the Copper River and rejected it in favor of Valdez, mostly because of the difficulty of getting past two glaciers, nose-to-nose, about 50 miles up the proposed Copper River route. Heney also learned that the Guggenheim engineers had neglected to file on the Copper River survey.

Heney and a few associates quietly disappeared up the Copper River to look it over.

The scene might have been out of the ice ages. Wind and noise assaulted the senses as two mighty glaciers faced each other in a gargantuan dance. The glaciers calved off icebergs, generating powerful tidal waves, and the bergs were then carried downstream on an extremely swift current. But the engineer with Heney pointed out that the glaciers were slightly offset and that a crossing could be made here, particularly if much of the work was done in winter when the glaciers were quiet.

RIGHT:

The builders of the Copper River & Northwestern Railroad pose for a November 1908 photo. Front row, left to right: James English, track superintendent; J.R. Van Cleve, superintendent; Sam Murchison, superintendent of construction; Michael J. Heney, contractor; Capt. "Dynamite" Johnny O'Brien, Alaska Steamship Co.; E.C. Hawkins, chief engineer; Alfred Williams (on step), assistant chief engineer; Dr. F.B. Whiting, chief surgeon; P. J. O'Brien, superintendent of bridges. Back row: Dr. W.W. Council, assistant surgeon; Archie Shiels; Bill Simpson; Mr. Robinson; and two unknowns. (E.A. Hegg; Anchorage Museum, Photo No. B72.104.3)

FAR RIGHT:

To build the Million Dollar Bridge, airtight chambers called caissons (center) allowed bridge builders to work underwater. Workers reached the caisson on a plank footbridge; compressed air was piped to the caisson through hoses strung beneath the catwalk. Work on the first pier with this caisson began in April 1909. The pier reached 36 feet below the riverbed and was completed Aug. 24. (Anchorage Museum, Photo No. B83.159.37)

Just beyond the proposed crossing was Abercrombie Rapids, formed by Miles Glacier squeezing against solid rock on the other side. This rock wall would be the only way through, for no one could build on the glacier face. There was a law that no single railroad could dominate any pass or canyon in Alaska, but Heney knew he had the key.

With a big Irish grin, Heney filed on the forgotten survey, told his powder monkeys to go up to Abercrombie, set dynamite, and wait. Then he began his own Copper River Railway from Cordova and offered to sell his route to the Guggenheims. Since it was one of their own rejected routes, they did not accept, but they did send a team up to look it over again. Their engineers were met by men warning them that they were preparing to blast and no one could enter the area. They were stopped cold.

The bluff worked. Within a year the Guggenheims bought out Heney's route — their own survey — for $250,000, and hired Heney as contractor to complete the Copper River &

Northwestern Railroad. Work began immediately, for copper ore was piling up at the Kennecott mine, ready for shipment.

From Cordova the railroad ran across delta wetlands to the first crossing of the Copper River, where transporting goods and men upriver became an incredible struggle. Lower Copper River is not navigable, so horses and supplies had to be lined upstream. One man stayed in the canoe or raft and steered, while the rest struggled through thick brush and rocks along the shore pulling on ropes, hauling the craft upstream. By this method, heavy equipment was transported ahead of the rails to the bridge site.

Building the Million Dollar Bridge at the glacier area was as difficult as they had predicted. All materials were of the heaviest type: caissons (underwater, air-tight excavation chambers) had to be sunk as far as 65 feet into the riverbed. Air hoses to the caissons were strung along a catwalk bridging the river, which also allowed men to cross if they had the nerve. Armored icebreakers were sunk on caissons to protect the piers.

Work had to go on above the site while the bridge itself was being built. A small sternwheeler was used in summer to take materials to the other side of the river, but tremendous waves from calving Miles Glacier continually washed out landings for it. In the winter, a sled-barge drawn by cable was used to transport goods, horses and men across, but it was far from efficient and was a danger to the caissons.

Hundreds of huge draft horses were needed to clear the railroad grade, and they had to be lined to Tiekel at Mile 100. In Woods Canyon, coyote holes — small tunnels to house dynamite for blasting — were driven into solid rock to gouge out a ledge for the trains to pass.

More than eight miles of bridges were built on the Copper River & Northwestern line, and all were steel except for the wooden trestle at Chitina. Each spring it washed away with the ice and was rebuilt. The recurring bridge washout was filmed for at least two movies: "The Days of '98" and "The Iron Trail." (Anchorage Museum, Photo No. B82.188.2)

To ease transportation problems, the steamship *Chitina* with its 5,700-pound boiler was taken over Tasnuna (Marshall) Pass by horse and sled, and assembled on the banks of the Copper River. From then on, moving supplies in the summer was a bit easier.

The Million Dollar Bridge crossing remained the greatest stumbling block to progress until its completion in spring 1910. The drama of its completion reads like a novel, and indeed became one by Rex Beach, *The Iron Trail* (1912). There were four spans, but the heaviest one was so big that it was originally designed to be built cantilever, i.e. two halves of the bridge were raised by cables and worked on independently, then lowered together and bolted in place.

But the bridge crossing was such a bottleneck, engineers decided to drive pilings through the ice in winter and build the huge span, weighing 5 million pounds, on this falsework. It was a good plan, but in midwinter the glaciers did the unthinkable: They began to move.

A glacier cannot be stopped. Ice 300 feet high and five miles across started pushing inexorably against river ice nine feet thick. Five million pounds of steel resting on a forest of pilings was gradually being pushed downstream. The gamble to finish the bridge before spring was being lost. One morning workers found the bridge was 18 inches out of line. Engineers huddled, and decided to put the cantilever into use. They raised the span, hauled it back into place by block and tackle and lowered it onto new pilings driven above the old.

Then the race was on to finish. In the dead of winter, men worked 30 hours around the clock in

a race with the glacier. Breakup was beginning; the bridge could be lost at any time. At last the final bolt was driven home, less than an hour before the ice went out. Workers stood watching in awe as the ice took the pilings away with a mighty roar. The Million Dollar Bridge was done. The railroad could be finished in less than a year.

But to reach Kennecott mine there were still three fairly large bridges to be built. The Kuskulana Bridge, until recently the highest in Alaska, was a cantilever-built steel span, constructed in winter

FACING PAGE:
The bridge across the Gilahina River was an 880-foot wooden trestle that took a half-million board feet of lumber. It was built January 1911, in subzero temperatures. The cold caused heavy timbers to crack apart when bolts were driven into them. (Jon R. Nickles)

LEFT:
The Kuskulana Bridge, at mile 146, was a cantilever-built steel span constructed amid the freezing, howling winds of winter 1910. After the railroad was abandoned, planking was put down for use by vehicular traffic. In spring 1988, the Alaska Department of Transportation laid a new deck with guard rails and replaced the approach trestles. Until recently the Kuskulana, at about 283 feet above the water, was the highest bridge in Alaska. (Anchorage Museum, Photo No. B83.159.49)

with temperatures of 50 below and winds blowing. Men were bundled in all the warm clothing they could find. The bridge's completion on New Year's Day 1911 was greeted with "the screeching of whistles, popping of guns, and lusty yells of the steelworkers," a fitting celebration for the new year.

The last large bridge was the high, curved Gilahina trestle, which even today, with portions of the center caved in, attracts photographers and tourists. Located at Mile 160, Gilahina is only 36 miles from the old Kennecott mine. The wooden bridge, whose pilings came from Pacific Coast forests, was 880 feet long, 80 to 90 feet high, and required half a million board feet of lumber. Gilahina is the only cambered trestle on the line. That is, it is curved and leans into its curve for a smooth train crossing.

Again it is the drama of its construction that

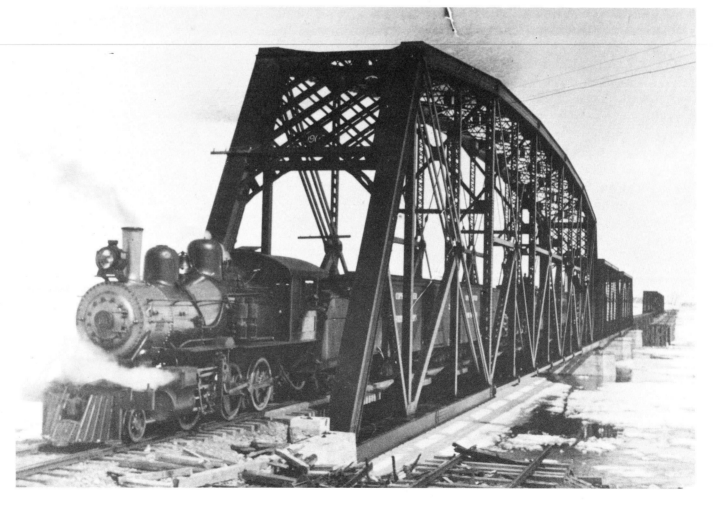

RIGHT:
A Copper River & Northwestern freight train crosses a bridge out of Cordova. The winds of the Copper River were so strong that, according to a story related by Lone Janson in The Copper Spike *(1975), a chain was fastened to the Flag Point Bridge at mile 27, and if the chain stuck out straight in the wind, trains did not cross. (Anchorage Museum, Photo No. B62.1.1472)*

FACING PAGE:
This aerial shows the remains of a railroad bridge across the braided Kennicott River west of McCarthy. (Steve McCutcheon)

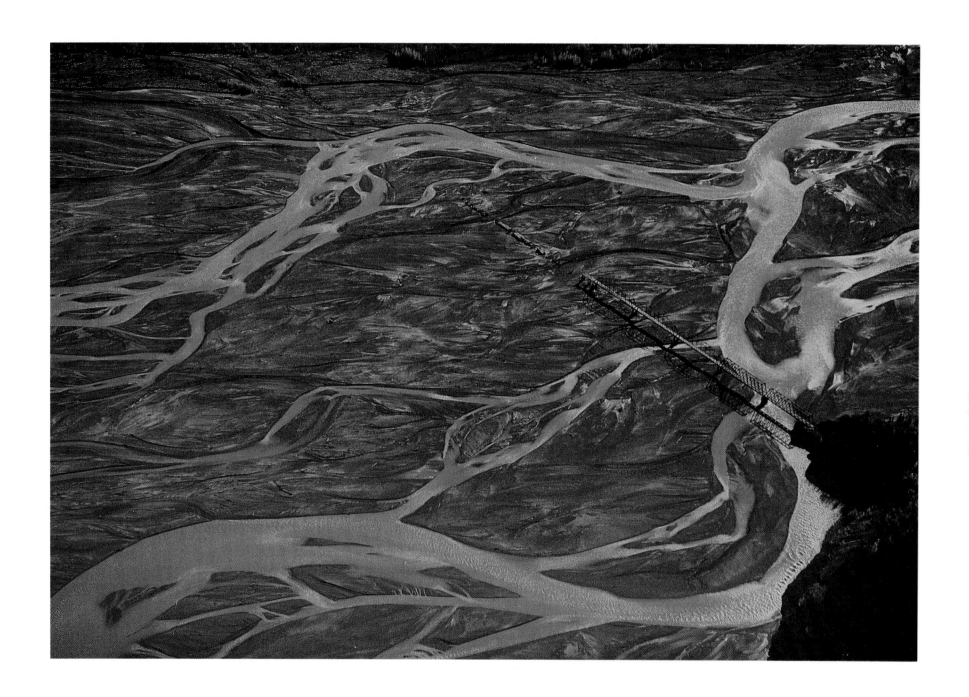

The Copper River & Northwestern followed the west bank of the Copper River from its mouth to Chitina, where the river is shown here. (Penny Rennick)

sets it apart. The bridge was constructed at temperatures from 30 to 60 below. In such cold, pilings could not be driven; holes had to be blasted into the frozen ground. Bolts could not be driven for the frozen pilings would split like matchsticks. Despite all this, the trestle was finished in record time, eight days.

Trains crossed Gilahina trestle on January 28, 1911, and exactly two months later, on March 28, 1911, the railroad was finished. Fittingly, it was completed by the driving of a copper spike instead of the traditional gold one. The ceremonial spike was fashioned from local copper from Chititu Creek, and suitably inscribed. After driving, it was redrawn and sent to S.W. Eccles, president of the line, in New York.

The Copper River crossing at Chitina was never finished. The trestle there was allowed to go out each spring and redriven next year. The recurring bridge washout became a favorite moviemakers' device; it was used in at least two movies: "The Days of '98" and "The Iron Trail." For the latter, it was to represent the pilings of the Million Dollar Bridge washing out.

Workers on the Copper River & Northwestern used to say that the railroad was built on snoose, overalls, whiskey and snowballs. Michael J. Heney, who came up through the ranks, understood that workers had few comforts, mostly snoose and whiskey. Heney once solved a difficult tunnel

The small Indian village of Eyak on Orca Bay was the site of an Alaska Packers Association salmon cannery when a survey party landed in 1906 to stake a route for Michael J. Heney's Copper River Railroad. Eyak had a deep-water anchorage and the cannery wharf and a small tramway had been bought by Heney. The men set up camp four miles up creek and nailed a sign on a tree that said "Cordova." The new town soon bustled with construction. Shown here is the original village, which became known as Old Eyak or Old Town. (Anchorage Museum, Photo No. B62.1.2193)

FACING PAGE:
Workers gather around while officials drive the final spike on the Copper River & Northwestern Railroad at Kennecott Mine Co.'s Bonanza Copper Mine in March 1911. Supt. John R. Van Cleve's private car with his guests, including E. C. Hawkins, chief engineer, had arrived at Kennecott the previous day, but a trestle and a final 800 feet of track needed to be readied before the spike-driving ceremony could take place. Hanging in a place of honor on the front of engine No. 50 is a photo of Michael J. Heney whose vision, energy and resolve assured completion of the line. Heney had died in the winter, a few months before the railroad was completed. (The Van Cleve Family, courtesy of Tim and Virgie McKeown)

construction problem by placing a case of whiskey at the other end, saying the whiskey belonged to the crew when they finished. The tunnel was completed in record time. Snoose was even more important to the workers, and Heney arbitrated an end to the only labor strike during construction, brought on by a shortage of snoose. The great Snoose Strike ended when Heney brought in a whole boxcar of snuff for the men.

The Copper River & Northwestern operated for 28 years, even through cold and deep snows, hauling copper, freight and tourists. 1916 was the big copper year, with more than $2 million per month flowing through Cordova. The Great Depression spelled the end; prices were down and Alaska operations expensive. The government would not allow the railroad to use coal underfoot, and there was no return cargo for the railroad. The last train puffed its way through Chitina in November 1939.

LEFT:
A locomotive coupled to four flatcars loaded with logs and a boxcar wait on the tracks just left of the depot at Chitina, an important stop on the Copper River & Northwestern. The town was nestled in a narrow valley near where the Chitina River flowed into the Copper. (Courtesy of Steve McCutcheon)

Going for the Gold:
Railroads Come to the Seward Peninsula

Editor's note: *This article is excerpted from "The Iron Horse Comes to the Peninsula," in Vol. 14, No. 3 of* ALASKA GEOGRAPHIC®, *Alaska's Seward Peninsula.*

The age of the automobile had not yet hit when the first waves of miners tackled the gold-bearing gravels on the Seward Peninsula. Costs of transporting supplies and equipment to various mines sometimes reached $200 to $300 per ton, enough to convince miners that a more efficient system was needed to carry weight and volume across the tundra. Railroads seemed the perfect solution, and as individual miners gave way to consolidated mining companies, a system of short railroads was built to rich mining sites.

Charles D. Lane, president of the Wild Goose Mining and Trading Co., led the drive for the first narrow-gauge railroad on the peninsula, named the Wild Goose. Lane convinced his Board of Directors that a track to the highly profitable Anvil Creek area, where the Wild Goose company alone had taken out $21 million in gold, would bring suitable rewards. By 1900, six and one-half miles of track ran from Nome to Anvil Mountain.

The Wild Goose lived up to Lane's claims, generating about $200,000 in revenue its first season. The line charged 2 cents per pound to haul freight. Round-trip passenger fare to the end of the line was $2; for 50 cents passengers could ride to Discovery on Lower Anvil Creek. Always looking for a new challenge, or perhaps his crystal ball gave him a hint of the future of gold-mining on the peninsula, Lane began selling his interests in the Wild Goose three years later. Under new ownership, the original Wild Goose became the Nome-Arctic line.

Wild Goose Mining and Trading Co. also had claims near Council, north and east of Nome. Seeing the success of his first railroad venture, Lane had a second Wild Goose line built to run from Council, then known as Council City, to a mine site at No. 15 Ophir Creek, about eight

FACING PAGE:
Rolling stock from the Council City and Solomon River Railroad lies weathering in the tundra near the community of Solomon on the Seward Peninsula. Southern terminus for the line was at Dickson, east across the Solomon River from the mining town. The remnants are close to the side of the Council Road out of Nome, and every year pieces disappear into the hands of souvenir collectors or scavengers. (Jon R. Nickles)

Tents for construction workers on the Seward Peninsula Railroad cluster at this camp near the junction of Iron Creek and Pilgrim River. Several miners found paying dirt along Iron Creek and looked to the railroad to lower their freight costs. The Seward Peninsula Railroad ran from Nome to Shelton on the Kuzitrin River. (Alaska Historical Library; photo by B.B. Dobbs)

miles from town. This line was also known as the Wild Goose, although officially it was the Golofnin Bay Railway Co.

Lane was not the only Seward Peninsula resident in the railroad business. J. Warren Dickson had his Council City and Solomon River Railroad, which started near the mining supply center of Solomon on the coast of Norton Sound and was to run inland to Council but never made it beyond mile 35. By 1903 Dickson had his crews working for $3 a day at the southern terminus, across the Solomon River from the mining community. Service was initiated in September, with $1 taking passengers to the end of the line 10 miles out near Big Hurrah Mine. Only 1,000 feet of track were laid

the following season, and to live up to its name the company established a stage line from the end of the track over the mountains to Council. The final year of construction, 1906, the line reached 35 miles to Penelope Creek. Dickson's dream never did come true, and as gold production declined in the area, so did the fortunes of the railroad.

About this time, gold production increased in the peninsula's interior, and miners in the Kougarok area clamored for cheaper freight rates. Once more promoters turned to the railroad. In 1906, the Seward Peninsula Railroad took over the Nome-Arctic track and extended the line in one season to Lane's Landing, later called Shelton, on the Kuzitrin River more than 80 miles inland and the southern gateway to the Kougarok.

The spongy tundra that created unstable roadbeds on the other lines also plagued the Seward Peninsula track. Passengers never knew when they might be called on to help hoist the train back onto the track. But a Sunday or holiday ride to the end of the line was great fun. During the height of operations, two trains daily made the run. Those with light loads reached Shelton in about 12 hours; the trip could take up to 20 hours if additional cars strained the locomotives.

Like the region's other railroads, the Seward Peninsula's revenues declined as gold production decreased. The line had a series of owners, including the Territory of Alaska, and was taken over and rehabilitated by the federal government. The federal Alaska Road Commission operated the line as a tram with provisions for draft animals and regulations to promote smooth traffic flow. Dogs pulled many of the loads in a wide array of vehicles, many of which were known as pupmobiles. When oncoming vehicles met on the single track, rules called for lighter loads to give way to heavier ones, and always on the uphill side, so that the operator could more easily put the wagon back on the tracks.

After World War II, Charles Reader ran a rail bus on the line, which he called the Curly Q, to take tourists to Salmon Lake. By the mid-1950s, however, the Nome-Taylor Road appropriated some of the railbed for its route, and the line was no longer used as a tram.

Numerous schemes have been proposed through the years to connect the Seward Peninsula by rail with the rest of Alaska and North America. Some even envisioned a tunnel under Bering Strait and a rail tie to Asia. Nomeite Jim Stimpfle, Alaska coordinator for the Interhemispheric Bering Strait Tunnel & Railroad Group formed in 1991, is pushing for the project, although he does not expect to see a tunnel in this century, he says.

Today scattered remnants of rolling stock and tracks lie weathering in the tundra, reminders of a time when railroads to the gold were seen as the solution to transportation problems for isolated mining camps on the Seward Peninsula.

Originally a station on the Wild Goose line built by Charles D. Lane in 1901, the Little Creek Station is now a stop on excursions offered by Nome Tour & Marketing. The Wild Goose has had an illustrious career on the Seward Peninsula. During World War II the military transported troops on the line, then the Nome city government took over operations to offer recreational opportunities for its citizens. In 1965 a Californian bought the line and removed the rails. Nomeites Wiley and Kitty Scott, owners of the tour company, have had the station for about five years. During visits, tourists can pan for gold, see reindeer and view a slide presentation in the station's little theater on the history of Nome and gold mining in the area. (Steve McCutcheon)

Tanana Valley Railroad

By Debbie S. Miller

Editor's note: *A longtime resident of Alaska's Interior and former teacher at Arctic Village, Debbie now lives in Fairbanks and is author of* Midnight Wilderness *(1990).*

In the early 1900s a tide of seasoned miners swept into the valleys that surround Fairbanks in search of gold. These prospectors had drifted to Alaska's Interior from the Klondike and Nome, hoping that the wave of gold strikes would continue along the Yukon River and its tributaries.

By 1904, hundreds of miners had staked claims along creeks such as Goldstream, Pedro, Vault, Little Eldorado and Gilmore. While winter trails were sufficient for horse-drawn sleds carrying heavy equipment and supplies to the mines, transporting materials in the summer was almost impossible. Only small quantities could be carried by pack animals across the muskeg.

Falcon Joslin, a Tennessee attorney and visionary who had successfully built 12 miles of railroad to the coal mines outside of Dawson City, Yukon Territory, offered a solution for the Fairbanks district miners. Backed initially by British investors, and later by U.S. companies, Joslin began construction of the first railroad in Alaska's Interior in 1905. By September, the first 25 miles of line were completed and operational.

First known as the Tanana Mines Railroad, the railway consisted of two lines. One spur of the narrow gauge ran from the community of Chena, near the confluence of the Chena and Tanana rivers, to Fairbanks. For a few years it was thought that Chena might become the urban center for the miners because of its deeper port on the larger Tanana River. When the Chena River was too low for riverboat passage, freight and passengers were delivered at Chena and brought 12 miles to Fairbanks by train. The second spur was constructed between Fairbanks and Fox, via Goldstream Valley, then north to the mining settlement of Gilmore.

FACING PAGE:
Engine No. 1 takes its place of honor outside the Fairbanks railroad depot in 1939. Originally built by the H.K. Porter Co. of Pittsburgh in March 1899, No. 1 was first used by the North American Transfer & Trading Co. of Vancouver, British Columbia. (M.P. Vogel, M.D.)

During construction of the railroad from Seward to Fairbanks, the federal government purchased the Tanana Valley Railroad, which had gone bankrupt in 1917. First known as the Tanana Mines Railroad, whose locomotive and passenger car are shown here, the line took on the name Tanana Valley Railroad in 1907. (Courtesy of Michael Nore)

Transporting railroad materials by steamship or riverboat from Canada was a considerable undertaking. Railroad equipment changed hands as many as 11 times en route to Fairbanks, and six flat cars sunk to the bottom of the Yukon River in one episode. Joslin wrote, "freight on the rails was more than twice their original cost, and much of the material was moved over six thousand miles."

Some of the equipment came from neighboring Yukon Territory. The Tanana Mines' first steam-driven locomotive was transported by riverboat from Whitehorse to Fairbanks after it was no longer needed on the White Pass and Yukon Railway. Other equipment was shipped by steamship from Seattle.

In 1907, an additional 20 miles of railroad was completed between Fox and the bustling mining community of Chatanika, 20 miles northeast of Fairbanks. This second stage of construction proved more difficult. As many as 200 construction workers, who reportedly earned $7.50 per day, initially planned to lay track between Gilmore and Chatanika via Cleary Summit.

Workers turned back when designers realized that the route's grade, along today's Steese Highway, was too steep for a railway. They looped the line back to Goldstream Creek and followed an easier northern route toward the settlements of Vault, Dome, Olnes and then on to Chatanika, the northern hub for mining. Several hundred people populated each of these busy settlements that no longer exist.

At summer's end in 1907, Fairbanks had grown to a booming mining town of 5,000 people. The 45-mile railroad was completed and renamed the Tanana Valley Railroad. With Judge James Wickersham presiding from Fairbanks, the golden spike was driven by Isabelle Barnette, wife of trader E.T. Barnette, founder of Fairbanks.

Between 1905 and 1910, the railroad received its most use. In 1908, Joslin reported that the railroad hauled 54,013 passengers and 14,666 tons of freight in the course of one year. The cost of freight ran 58 cents per ton per mile, while freight delivered by teams of horses cost $3.00 per ton per mile. Joslin was proud of the fact that the railroad saved people as much as $300,000 each year in freight costs.

Dr. Nicholas Deely, a Fairbanks pediatrician with a fascination for trains, has extensively studied the history of railroading in Alaska and written two photographic books on the Alaska Railroad. Dr. Deely pointed out that in its heyday, the Tanana

Curt Fortenberry (left) and Pat Durand, foreman of the restoration project, work on Engine No. 1. Friends of the Tanana Valley Railroad Inc., a non-profit corporation, has formed to recover and restore the engine and other artifacts relating to the Tanana Valley Railroad. (Courtesy of Friends of the Tanana Valley Railroad)

Dr. Nicholas Deely (in white), a Fairbanks pediatrician, works with members of Friends of the Tanana Valley Railroad hauling out old narrow gauge track that still can be found in a few places. The track will be cut up and sold to raise money for restoration of Engine No. 1. (Courtesy of Friends of the Tanana Valley Railroad)

The locomotives usually hauled several cars, both freight and passenger, and that sometimes caused a problem because of federal restrictions on hazardous freight. Dynamite was commonly used at the mining camps, but the law required that the explosive be kept at a safe distance from passenger cars. Because the Tanana Valley train was relatively short with mixed freight and passengers cars, it could not meet the regulation.

"To meet the safety requirement the dynamite supplies were separated. The freight cars carried the sticks, and the passengers rode with the caps," Deely said, noting that Alaska has always been faced with federal regulations that are often not suited for a frontier way of life.

The Tanana Valley Railroad also had its share of struggles operating in the northern climate. In the winter there would be weeks with no train service because tracks were drifted with snow or plastered with ice. Trains were sometimes stranded, and dog teams occasionally rescued passengers who were stuck en route. Spring brought considerable flooding in Goldstream Valley, and it was not uncommon for rails to be completely submerged. Conductors wore hip boots during breakup and probed the rail bed with a long pole to be sure the tracks and ties had not washed away.

With the early success of the Tanana Valley Railroad, Joslin had a vision that a network of railroads would be built linking Fairbanks, Nome and Circle City to a port at Haines. He felt that 10,000 miles of railroads were ultimately needed in Alaska to adequately develop the resources. He summed up this need in 1908 when he wrote:

"...Nearly every man in Alaska has a claim, lying

Valley Railroad served its most important purpose by hauling mining equipment and supplies to the mining camps, and bringing wood back to Fairbanks to fuel the sternwheelers, the Northern Commercial Co. power plant and the train itself. But the railroad also provided regular passenger service for mining families twice a day.

Just as today, Fairbanks was the center for cultural, sporting and holiday events, and the place where mining families did their shopping.

"Mining families from the outlying communities regularly came to Fairbanks for grocery shopping, baseball games, indoor hockey, doctor appointments and holiday events, like the Fourth of July," Deely said.

practically inaccessible. Only a narrow fringe along navigable water has been partially developed yet this fringe is producing 40 million dollars a year in trade with the States. The population is about forty thousand, and probably shows the highest ratio of production of any people in the world...."

Although the Nome-to-Haines network of railways never came to pass, Joslin was instrumental in convincing Congress to appropriate funds to build 1,000 miles of railroad. In 1923, the Alaska Railroad, a federal project, was completed between Fairbanks and Seward.

During the 1910s, it became increasingly difficult to operate the mining camps because of fuel shortages. Each year miners had to travel farther to chop wood to fuel the boilers they used to melt permafrost and unearth gold deposits. As mining activity diminished, trucks began carrying the smaller quantities of supplies for the camps, and there was less demand for the railway.

To lower the heavy cost of fuel for the train, Joslin purchased a battery-operated locomotive for

A Tanana Valley Railroad train stops to take on wood, burned to power the steam engines. The bridge over Fox Gulch shows in the distance. (Archives, Alaska and Polar Regions Department, University of Alaska; Falcon Joslin Album #2, Photo No. 79-41-66N)

A branch of the Tanana Valley Railroad connected Fairbanks to the mining community of Chatanika. The 20-mile spur ran through the mining camps of Fox and Gilmore. This view of the Fox station shows men, probably miners, with their wagons and teams of horses waiting for the train. (Archives, Alaska and Polar Regions Department, University of Alaska; Falcon Joslin Album #2, Photo No. 79-41-52N)

passenger and light freight service. The $38,000 Edison electric locomotive, transported by steamship from Seattle, was the first of its kind to operate west of the Rockies. Publicity claimed that the locomotive could carry 30 passengers at 30 mph, and run 360 miles without recharge. Joslin calculated that it cost two-thirds of one cent per kilowatt to operate the electric trolley, about half the cost of running a wood-fired steam engine. The electric trolley provided convenient commuter service between Fox, the University of Alaska at College, and Fairbanks until 1930.

In 1917, with the decline of mining activity and the increased competition from trucks for

During the 1920s, the line between Fairbanks and Nenana was gradually widened to standard gauge. The narrow-gauge spur to Fox and Chatanika operated until 1930, after which it was torn up and the material used elsewhere.

Although the Tanana Valley Railroad no longer exists, there is still interest in the railroad's history. Friends of the Tanana Valley Railroad, a group of 50 railroad enthusiasts in Fairbanks, are restoring Engine No. 1, the first and last steam-powered engine used on the line. Narrow-gauge track that will accommodate the engine already exists at Alaskaland theme park in Fairbanks. Dan Gullickson, president of the organization, said there are plans for a railroad museum that will include historical photographs and railroad artifacts.

Although the tracks are gone, and the days of steam-powered engines puffing toward Chatanika are past, the Tanana Valley Railroad will be remembered as an essential transportation network for early pioneers.

freight, the Tanana Valley Railroad went bankrupt, and was sold to the federal government. The rails were removed from the Chena-Fairbanks line and used in the construction of a narrow-gauge track between Fairbanks and Nenana. This feeder line connected with the Alaska Railroad's main line to Seward.

Dynamite and Gandy Dancers:
The Alaska Railroad

The whistle sounds and a train thunders into sight. Children in Elderberry Park, on a hill above the tracks in downtown Anchorage, scramble atop the slide for a better view. Some wave, and an engineer flicks his hand from a window in the blue and gold locomotive. Everyone in the park seems transfixed by the tons of rumbling iron and steel, and they watch until the train disappears around a curve. Along 535 miles of track, from the northern terminal town of Fairbanks in the Interior to the southcentral seaports of Whittier and Seward, Alaska Railroad trains roll with spellbinding power.

Trains captivate people of all ages, and for good reason. They are big and noisy, they carry all sorts of things, and they represent progress, civilization on the move. They harken to those early days of putting people and towns where there were none, lacing vast stretches of wilderness with trestles, tunnels and track. While politicians and visionaries plotted the future, gandy dancers punched through the line. These laborers, mostly foreign immigrants, thousands of men and a few women, performed backbreaking and dangerous work. They blasted rock, shoveled dirt, wrestled rail and swung the mauls that drove the spikes for the transportation network that developed the nation.

The turn of the century brought the iron horse to Alaska, to open the nation's most northern lands to prospectors, miners, homesteaders and tourists. The Alaska Railroad was not the territory's first, but it was the most influential and enduring railway. For much of its 77-year history, it was the only railroad in the nation built and operated by the federal government. It created what became Alaska's largest city, Anchorage, and spurred growth of numerous other communities, including Seward, Fairbanks, Nenana and Talkeetna.

Today's Alaska Railroad Corp. is a profitable venture offering modern freight-handling capabilities as well passenger service from Fairbanks to Seward and Whittier. Since its transfer to the state in 1985, about $100 million has been spent

FACING PAGE:
A train of empty coal cars, powered by six Alaska Railroad diesels, heads north along Turnagain Arm from Seward, returning to Usibelli Coal Mine in the Interior. Some of the steepest grade on the line occurs in the Chugach Mountains between Portage and Seward, and five to six engines are required to supply enough horsepower to pull a heavy coal train. At two points through the mountains, the coal train is divided and the engines pull half the train up the grade, then return for the second half in a maneuver known as "doubling the hill." (John W. Warden)

A gas car ran once or twice weekly during the summers on the Alaska Northern Railway from Seward to mile 47. This photograph was taken in 1910 at Bear Creek. The Alaska Northern started out in 1903 as the Alaska Central, a meagerly financed venture that went bankrupt in 1909, was reorganized as the Alaska Northern and had been extended to Kern Creek at the head of Turnagain Arm by the time the government bought it. The route to Fairbanks originally surveyed by the Alaska Central's promoters was essentially the same one adopted by the Alaskan Engineering Commission for the government railroad. (Anchorage Museum, Photo No. B 62.1.1482)

upgrading the line and equipment, from replacing track to computerizing the books. In an industry trend, cabooses are being phased out as electronic "defect detectors" are installed along the track to monitor passing cars for problems. They report almost instantaneously in an odd-sounding computerized voice to the train's engineer. In 1990, new passenger coaches went into service, the first brand-new passenger equipment in the railroad's history. As a federally owned line, it had received mostly used and refurbished equipment bought from other lines and governments. Despite

all its modernization, the Alaska Railroad still offers an old-time convenience to rural residents along the railbelt: It is the only railroad in North America that still has flag stops, where trains stop when folks want to get on or off at remote sites along the line.

The Alaska Railroad, or the Government Railroad as it was known in its early years, came about after years of agitation for a railroad to link the territory's mineral and timber deposits to a seaport. In 1912, the U.S. Congress authorized creation of the Alaska Railroad Commission. The four-member commission recommended a two-pronged railroad from the coastal towns of Cordova and Seward to the bawdy gold-mining town of Fairbanks. After much debate, Congress finally agreed in 1914 to fund $35 million for the federal railroad construction and operation. President Woodrow Wilson appointed three men to the Alaska Engineering Commission: western railroader William Edes; Frederick Mears, fresh off

construction of the Panama Canal; and Thomas Riggs Jr., who later became governor of Alaska. The commission was in charge of surveying and construction. Survey parties traversed variations of the proposed routes by horseback, on foot and in canoes, picking their way across glaciers, fighting mosquito-infested muskeg and fording icy rivers. Within a year, they were back in Washington with

This view shows the interior of the District Engineer's office at Dead Horse Camp on March 7, 1919. This was the railroad's construction headquarters for the Talkeetna District. (Anchorage Museum, Photo No. AEC G-1181)

A welcome stop on the Alaska Railroad was the hotel at Curry, 20 miles north of Talkeetna on the east bank of the Susitna River. Known during earlier railroad construction days as Dead Horse Camp, the settlement's name was changed to Curry in 1922 to honor Charles Forrest Curry, a Congressman from California. Curry's renown even attracted honeymooners, who would overnight in the hotel (at left) and then join other visitors in an outing across the bridge and up Curry Ridge on the opposite side of the river. (Steve McCutcheon)

Horses pull dinky No. 4 on sled runners toward Riley Creek on Feb. 17, 1921. The bridges at Hurricane Gulch, over Riley Creek and across the Tanana River at Nenana were the last gaps in the Alaska Railroad track. The first steel for the Riley Creek span was laid in late fall 1921; on Feb. 5, 1922, the entire span was in place. The 701-foot single span over the Nenana was, at the time, the longest bridge span in the United States. (Anchorage Museum, Photo No. T 201)

seven proposals for the President's consideration.

The people of Cordova saw their town as a good choice for the new railroad. Already the Copper River & Northwestern Railroad connected Cordova with the rich Kennecott copper mine, and extending this line on to Fairbanks with a spur to the Bering River coal field seemed a logical move. This line was offered for sale to the government by its owners, the rich and powerful J.P. Morgan and Guggenheim families. But the Morgan-Guggenheim syndicate were seen as a political liability, having been part of a national scandal over alleged illegal claims in the Bering River coal field, a scandal that helped bring down President William Howard Taft's previous administration. Whether it was political pressure against the government buying the Copper River & Northwestern, or whether it was, as some have suggested, personal animosity toward the Morgan-Guggenheim clan, President Wilson chose only one route, out of Seward.

Seward had its own railroad, the Alaska Northern Railway Co., headed toward Fairbanks, but it had only reached 71 miles to Kern Creek on Turnagain Arm when the federal government started building its railroad in 1915. A group of

Seattle businessmen had built a terminal and laid some track for the Alaska Central Railway out of Seward in 1904, but financial problems resulted in its takeover by Alaska Northern six years later. The government eventually paid $1,157,339 for the line. At the north end, the government bought the 45-mile narrow gauge Tanana Valley Railroad for $300,000.

Construction of the new railroad started where Ship Creek empties into Knik Arm of Cook Inlet, and practically overnight a tent city sprang up on the flats by the creek. The first town lots were auctioned in July and the citizens of this new government town eventually named it Anchorage. The first spike was driven on April 29, 1915, and

throughout the summer, material and equipment used in building the recently opened Panama Canal were delivered to Seward. Thousands of men looking for work poured into the port at Seward and made their way to the main camp at Ship Creek. Construction proceeded north and south through the mostly unpopulated wilderness. Supplies were transported by train to the end of the track, freighted overland along snow-roads and frozen rivers during winter, or delivered in summer by boats traveling Turnagain and Knik arms and the Susitna and other rivers into the Interior.

The construction camps that sprang up along the route resembled small towns of tents, crudely built log buildings, docks, machine shops, sawmills,

This trestle bridge at mile 48 was one of five that made up the famous Loop to overcome a steep grade between Grandview, mile 44, and Tunnel, mile 51. The Loop was designed by Frank Bartlett, locating engineer for the old Alaska Central Railway, and included a four-story loop that circled back on itself on high trestles to avoid costly sidehill and tunnel work. The Loop was bypassed with a new route in 1951. (Anchorage Museum, Photo No. B 87.71.47)

and hospitals. The bunkhouses were divided into honeycomblike cells about four feet tall called muzzleloaders. They were barely big enough for a pole bed and a couple of duffel bags. Baseball quickly became a favorite pastime, with section crews playing each other and commission teams. Some of the first excursion trains carried fans to games up and down completed sections of track.

By 1917, the railroad's construction crews peaked at 4,500 workers. The work included miles of heavy rock excavation and tunneling, particularly the 30 miles of grade along the shoreline of Turnagain Arm between Kern and Potter. Feats of audacious engineering abounded, among them bridges across the Susitna and Tanana rivers and Hurricane Gulch. The famous Loop was another, a spiral of track that wound across five trestle bridges and through a heated tunnel. It was located between Grandview, at 1,060 feet the highest point on the railroad's route

The Alaska Railroad operates "Express" passenger service daily between Anchorage and Fairbanks with stops in Wasilla, Talkeetna and Denali National Park. In 1988 this new passenger depot, built with spruce logs from Alaska's Kenai Peninsula, opened in Denali. (John W. Warden)

through the Kenai Mountains, and Tunnel at mile 51. An expensive stretch to maintain, costing about $36,000 a year, the Loop was constantly besieged by snow slides and icy rails in winter. In 1951, the Loop was bypassed with a new section of track, a rerouting that became possible because Bartlett Glacier had retreated a mile in the 30 years since the original line was laid.

During the construction years, the government railroad had far-reaching powers. It was responsible for securing supplies, selling town lots, building power plants, hospitals and public schools. It provided a market and transportation for coal mined from the Matanuska Valley and Nenana regions. It promoted tourism in the territory with full-color brochures. It operated a hotel at Mount McKinley National Park as well as a railside resort at Curry, in the Talkeetna Mountains, with a 75-room hotel, tennis courts, swimming pool, three-hole golf course and a ridge-top lookout called Regalvista from which Mount McKinley could be

(continued, page 52)

FACING PAGE:
A train carrying autos from Whittier emerges from a tunnel near Portage into an avalanche chute. Snow has been cleared from the tracks. The Alaska Railroad Corp. and the Alaska Department of Transportation work together in an avalanche control program. Avalanche zones are monitored for threatening snowslide conditions, at which time the road or track is closed to traffic and an avalanche is created on purpose by firing a 105mm recoilless rifle at the mountain. (John W. Warden)

LEFT:
Luggage for tourists visiting Denali National park is unloaded at the Alaska Railroad depot. The number of people riding the Alaska Railroad has steadily increased from about 250,000 in 1985 to 471,217 in 1991. (Harry M. Walker)

"I Worked to Survive"

By Jeffrey R. Richardson

For Alice Norton swinging a 9-pound hammer was not a political statement, it was survival. At 92 cents an hour, the work was an important boost to her family.

Right after World War II, Norton and eight other Athabaskan women from Cantwell near Broad Pass in the Alaska Range were hired on as gandy dancers by the Alaska Railroad on the Cantwell Section. Still short of men, many of whom had enlisted or left the railroad for higher-paying civilian jobs, company officials had trouble finding laborers to do essential track maintenance.

Along with Norton, the Cantwell female crew included Lucille, Olga and Valdez Tyone; Yaddy, Mary and Helen Stickivan; Grace Secondchief and Jane Tansy.

Hugh Jones, section foreman, had ample opportunity to observe both his male and female crew and later praised the women as quick learners and hard workers: "I never saw anyone that could do as neat a job of dressing track as Helen Stickivan did, she was really first class. They were all good spikers and seldom missed a spike or broke a maul handle. They could do a good job of tamping ties and most any of it except the

Shortly after World War II, a group of female Athabaskan gandy dancers joined the crew in charge of maintaining a section of the Alaska Railroad track near Cantwell. The quartet closest to the photographer includes (from left) Valdez Tyone, Alice Norton, Grace Secondchief and Helen Stickivan. (Anchorage Museum, Photo No. BL 79.2.3503)

very heavy lifting, except for Grace and Alice and possibly Mary."

For some of the women, wartime cessation of gold mining in Alaska had created economic hardship. Others came from families with no other breadwinners. Norton was supporting her five children and two other household members, recalls one of her daughters Maggie Oliver.

"Mom hunted and trapped along with working to keep us going. I remember when they'd have a derailment and they'd work till it was fixed and she'd just come dragging home," says Oliver.

Although Cantwell's female gandy dancers were only on the payroll for about six years, they earned a solid, no-nonsense reputation for both their professional and personal demeanor. Some years back, the story was recounted of a conductor who habitually swatted the women with his glove as the train went by. Tiring of this harassment, one of the women eventually grabbed the offending conductor by the wrist and yanked him end-over-end off the train.

Members of the Cantwell crew standing in front of the section tool house in 1948 were, left to right, Jake Tansy, Lucille Tyone, Alice Norton, John Nicklie, Pete Tyone, Yaddy Stickivan, Mary Stickivan and Oley Nicklie. (Anchorage Museum, Photo No. BL 79.2.2563)

Alice Norton, last of the female crew, lived until 1986. She had become well-known up and down the Alaska Railroad as Cantwell Alice, and her daughter remembers the affection shown her and her siblings for many years by the train crews.

Coming upon work crews in her later years, Cantwell Alice would often stop and size up their work, says Oliver. "She used to tease other workers, tell them 'You've got a kink down there.' Tell them what was wrong."

Neither Norton nor the other female crew swung mauls and hefted ties to prove a point. Although the upsurge in feminism eventually brought her public notoriety, Norton would counter the attention with a terse retort: "What do you mean women's lib? I worked to survive."

By the time she died, the Alaska Railroad had new owners, but Norton and her sisters were not forgotten. Standing by her casket was a special memorial sent by the railroad, a 9-pound hammer.

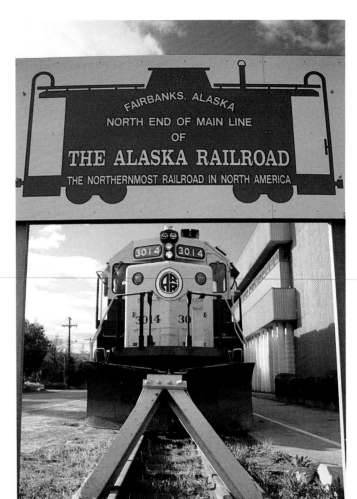

seen. The railroad promoted agriculture, for a time employing an agricultural development agent. It operated a creamery for butter and ice cream, and a portable cannery car to introduce new food preservation techniques to homesteaders, selling the excess canned goods in railroad commissaries.

On July 15, 1923, eight years and some $60 million after construction began, President Warren G. Harding drove the golden spike to complete the railroad in ceremonies at Nenana, then one of the territory's largest towns. By 1938, under management of Col. Otto F. Ohlson, the Alaska Railroad for the first time turned a profit. From then on, it never required a Congressional appropriation for operating expenses.

World War II brought a boom to the railroad. In 1940, the railroad was called to transport tons of construction supplies and thousands of soldiers as the military fortified the territory, building Air Force and Army bases in Anchorage and Fairbanks. The railroad's traffic increased, but its work force decreased as employees joined the military. In 1943, the shortage became so critical that 1,150 men of the 714th Railway Operating Battalion were assigned to the Alaska Railroad.

In the meantime the military, worried about a bottleneck occurring at the port in Seward, funded construction of a 12-mile rail spur from Portage through the Chugach Mountains to the ice-free port of Whittier. This became the military's fuel depot, a spot well concealed from possible enemy attack by its remote location at the head of Passage Canal and its frequently lousy weather. Today the Whittier spur is one of the most heavily traveled sections of the Alaska Railroad, transporting about 150,000 people a year and all freight entering and leaving the state by way of rail barges. These barges, fitted with track, link the Alaska Railroad with railroads in the Lower 48 and Canada; freight cars roll off and on rail barges at the Alaska Railroad siding in Whittier for transport to and from Seattle and Prince Rupert, British Columbia. Along with these freight cars, the Whitter train includes numerous flatbeds to carry autos, motor homes,

UNITED STATES

DENALI

HARDING CAR
DENALI
USED BY PRESIDENT WARREN G. HARDING
ON HIS TRIP TO ALASKA IN 1923
TO DRIVE THE GOLDEN SPIKE FOR THE
ALASKA RAILROAD. DENALI IS THE
INDIAN NAME FOR "MT McKINLEY,
THE GREAT ONE."

fishing boats and tour buses; Whittier is the closest fishing port on Prince William Sound to Anchorage as well as a connection point with the state ferry from Valdez. Most of the people who travel the Whittier shuttle just drive their vehicle up a ramp and onto the train, for a slow, sideways rocking ride that passes through two lovely valleys and two dark tunnels, including one 13,890 feet long, one of the longest railroad tunnels in the United States.

After the war, the railroad was practically worn out. Although the railroad's detractors in Congress

FAR LEFT:
This is the springtime view looking east toward the Talkeetna Mountains from the middle of the railroad span nearly 300 feet above Hurricane Gulch. One of the Alaska Railroad's diesel cars had stopped on the span, and passengers had an unobstructed view of the gulch. (Penny Rennick)

LEFT:
The 1964 earthquake caused about $30 million damage to the Alaska Railroad, with the heaviest damage concentrated at Seward, Whittier, along Turnagain Arm and in Anchorage. This aerial shows the destruction at Portage, where the Whittier spur joins the mainline. The earthquake destroyed the town of Portage and dropped the land 4 to 10 feet in the Portage area and along Turnagain Arm. The tracks were rebuilt above flood level, but the town was abandoned and the railroad station building sold at a salvage price of $7,000. Today, a large parking lot at Portage serves as a transfer point for passengers and motorists taking the train to Whittier. (Steve McCutcheon)

and new 115-pound steel rail replaced most of the lighter weight track. A continued shortage of workers resulted in the government flying crews of Eskimos in from western Alaska. In Cantwell, nine Athabaskan women joined a section crew, working on the line from 1945 to 1950.

From its beginning, the Alaska Railroad has been besieged with weather-related operational and maintenance problems. In summer, the long, warm days bring about lush vegetation that obscures the tracks and undermines the roadbeds. The railroad would like to douse the weeds with herbicides, but have been stopped by people worried about the possible environmental consequences. So work crews chop down the weeds by hand. Other times, avalanches, ice-coated rails, floods, and thawing and freezing ground that buckles tracks cause problems,

had at one time wanted the line abandoned, the railroad's performance during the war seemed to ensure its continuation. Alaska was at the forefront in the newly brewing Cold War with Russia, and there was already talk in Congress of Alaska statehood. The massive reconstruction was approved, at a cost of nearly $100 million. Some of the wooden river bridges were replaced with steel,

The Alaska's Railroad's 50th anniversary was celebrated July 15, 1973, with a gold spike ceremony at the north end of the Nenana River bridge. Retired railroad foreman Sam Chamis (front left with hat) and Alaska Railroad Manager Walter Johnson (behind Chamis) advise a federal transportation official on spike-driving techniques. This spike was driven at the same spot where President Warren G. Harding drove the first golden spike in 1923. (Steve McCutcheon)

sometimes shutting down traffic and causing derailments. Fortunately few people in Alaska have died from train accidents. However there have been train related injuries and industrial damages. In March 1986, a leaking chemical tank car at Crown Point, on the Kenai Peninsula, resulted in the evacuation of local residents and cost the railroad about $650,000 to clean up affected homes and pay for the displacement. In 1990, a 70-car train derailed near Dunbar, between Nenana and Fairbanks, and some 160,000 gallons of diesel and jet fuel spilled from seven ruptured tank cars. Within three weeks, the railroad had cleaned up most of the spill.

Nor has the railroad escaped natural disasters. The Good Friday earthquake of 1964 did about $30 million in damage, mostly along the railroad's southern leg and its facilities in Seward and Whittier. Submarine land slides in the port of Seward collapsed the docks and shoreside terminal facilities, plunging a five-story crane into the water so completely that divers never found a trace.

Seismic waves that followed destroyed a loaded freight train and crushed fuel tanks that ignited. Steel rails along Turnagain Arm in some places were twisted into great curves; in other places they snapped in two and remained suspended in mid-air, five and six feet above subsided earth. The Army shipped a giant floating crane to Whittier, to replace destroyed freight unloading facilities. Railroad employees worked untold hours rebuilding demolished track. Within 10 days, traffic was restored on the least damaged part of the line between Anchorage and Fairbanks, and within three weeks the first train since the earthquake traveled over temporary track from Whittier to Anchorage, hauling much needed supplies from Outside. By September, temporary repairs allowed the first freight train to run from Anchorage to Seward, but it was two years before new railroad docks, warehouse and terminal in Seward were reopened and reconstruction was complete.

In October 1986, a 100-year flood knocked out two major bridges and several smaller ones north of Wasilla, covering tracks in mud and causing nearly $3 million in damage. Service was restored in 13 days.

A problem the railroad may never solve is that of moose on the tracks, particularly in winter when the cleared roadbed is an attractive alternative to belly-deep snow. The railroad cuts through prime moose habitat in many places, and collisions with

FAR LEFT:
Laborers who built the Alaska Railroad used brass plates to draw their pay from the Alaskan Engineering Commission. This one belonged to H.H. McCutcheon, who worked on the railroad in 1916. (Steve McCutcheon)

LEFT:
Conductor Steve Culver greets a passenger getting off an Alaska Railroad train in Denali National Park. (Harry M. Walker)

the giant ungulates are inevitable. In 1990, a record number of 722 moose, weakened by severe cold and heavy snowfall, were killed by trains. Railroaders have tried all sorts of remedies to move moose off the tracks. Once in the 1950s, an exasperated brakeman placed a flare under the tail of a moose found sleeping on the track; it bolted

but the incident brought a flood of protest letters from animal lovers. More recently, the railroad has plowed wider berms, to give moose cleared paths other than the track, and sends a rail-fitted truck ahead of the trains to shoo moose away.

In 1991, the Alaska Railroad entered into real estate development, a venture new to the state-owned corporation but rooted in the beginnings of the federal railroad. A new hotel, built by a Spokane, Wash., firm on railroad property along Ship Creek in downtown Anchorage, opened in summer 1992 primarily to serve railroad passengers. The hotel is expected to anchor the 120-acre Ship Creek Redevelopment Project with which the railroad wants to turn its industrial property near the Anchorage rail yard into retail and tourist attractions. As part of this, the railroad moved its business offices into another new building,

RIGHT:
A southbound Alaska Railroad train exits a tunnel above the Nenana River, north of Denali National Park near Lynx Creek. The stretch of track through the canyon, which parallels the river and hugs mountainsides, is difficult to maintain because of the terrain, high winds, cold temperatures, deep snow, spring runoff and heavy fall rains. It was also difficult to build. E. J. Cronin, who worked on the railroad during that time, likened the hardships of completing the project to those encountered by the Pharaohs of Egypt in building the pyramids. (John W. Warden)

FAR RIGHT:
Section crews use small gasoline-powered cars, like this one parked on rail siding near Girdwood, to inspect track. (Diamond Arts Photography)

White spruce loaded at Nenana travels by rail about 400 miles to the port at Seward for export to Japan, where it is used for houses and chopsticks. (Steve McCutcheon)

modeled after a Pacific Northwest railroad depot, erected on railroad property by a private developer and leased back to the railroad corporation. Hundreds of parcels of railroad property are leased by various companies, but the project along Ship Creek is the first time the corporation has actively sought to develop its land.

From steam engine No. 556 parked on the Delaney Park Strip in downtown Anchorage, to the sidelined sleeping coaches that make up part of the accommodations at Denali National Park Hotel, to the retired Pullman dining car that serves as a summertime visitor center in Seward, pieces of Alaska Railroad's history mingle with modern-day operations, part of a continuum of the railroad's participation in the development of Alaska.

Railroads in Alaska:
An Economic Lifeline

By Rose Ragsdale

Editor's note: An Anchorage economics and business writer, Rose works part time for the Alaska Journal of Commerce *and writes and edits a quarterly newsletter,* LOOK Alaska, *which explores how to solve Alaska's problems and is sponsored by Alyeska Pipeline Service Co.*

Modern-day railroading in Alaska is small potatoes in a world of giants.

A scant 535 miles of track on main and branch lines provides rail transportation for a state that could swallow two of Texas with room left over for Alabama. Yet the state-owned railroad system is a lifeline for Alaska's $25 billion economy.

The Alaska Railroad extends from the ice-free ports of Whittier and Seward on the Gulf of Alaska to Fairbanks in the Interior. The tracks tunnel through a mountain range before hugging the shores of Cook Inlet. Past Anchorage, they crawl through the Matanuska and Susitna valleys and skirt the eastern edge of Denali National Park before descending into Fairbanks. Along their path lies the "railbelt," home to three-quarters of Alaska's 550,000 residents.

The railroad fulfills its original mission by linking mining, timber and petroleum resources in Alaska's Interior with economical water transportation to remote villages and export markets. In 1991, it shipped 5.1 million tons of freight, including exports of coal for Korea, logs for Japan and fish for Canada. It also brought consumer goods and petroleum products to growing urban centers, while transporting oil field supplies bound for the Arctic or points along the 800-mile trans-Alaska pipeline.

A spur to development, the Alaska Railroad has grown along with the state. Today, it operates 55 locomotives, 1,224 freight cars and 28 passenger cars on 483 miles of main line, 52 miles of branch line and 126 miles of yards and sidings. Based in Anchorage, the railroad has 611 employees, of

FACING PAGE:
Railroad cars take on gravel at Palmer. Gravel is the Alaska Railroad's largest commodity by weight of shipment, and in 1991 the line hauled 1.8 million tons to Anchorage distributors from suppliers in the Matanuska and Susitna valleys. (Sean Reid)

An Alaska Railroad passenger train crosses Riley Creek bridge in Denali National Park. The silver cars belong to private tour companies that contract with the railroad for carrier service. (John W. Warden)

which 482 are members of five unions. Workers earn wages adjusted slightly higher than those paid for comparable jobs in the Lower 48 to offset the added costs of living in Alaska. The railroad collected $68.3 million in total revenue in 1991, including $51.9 million from its freight operations. It also showed a profit of $4.4 million.

To purchase the railroad from the federal government in 1985, the state paid $22.3 million and spent $10.9 million in start-up expenses. Since then, the railroad has earned a profit every year, except in 1986 when storms washed out several bridges and nearly 200 miles of track and shut down the system for almost two weeks.

Today, the railroad competes with trucking companies and barge lines, but still enjoys a solid clientele for basic commodities and a growing demand for consumer goods and passenger service.

Coal is the railroad's primary international export commodity. It shipped 1.3 million tons in 1991 that generated nearly $12 million, or an average of about $9 a ton, in freight revenue. The coal is extracted from Usibelli Coal Mine at Healy and about half of it is shipped by Korea-based Suneel Corp. south to Seward where it is loaded onto ships bound for Korea Electric Power Co. The remaining output is shipped north to Clear Air Force Station and to outlets near Fairbanks.

The railroad's involvement with Usibelli's efforts to export coal began in the early 1980s when the railroad was still under federal ownership. It was an example of how railroads could foster development, observers say. Suneel wanted to buy the coal and move it by rail to a port in Anchorage or Whittier. But the Korean company finally chose Seward because federal railroad officials offered it a 55-year lease on seven acres of land near the port.

Next, the railroad purchased five locomotives and 80 coal hopper cars to haul the coal from Healy to Seward. In 1984 the state Department of Transportation completed dredge and dock work in Seward. The next year, as railroad ownership transferred to the state, ownership of the dock facility was transferred to the state-owned railroad corporation.

Other commodities with export potential are also handled by the railroad.

Forest products, for example, are a small fraction of the railroad's total freight load. But customers such as ITT Rayonier are shipping millions of board feet of cottonwood, spruce and birch logs by rail from Nenana and Fairbanks to Asian markets where the lumber is gaining popularity in home construction.

The railroad's largest commodity by weight of shipments is gravel, with 1.8 million tons

A freight train passes a passenger train at the Healy siding. Sidings allow the railroad to run both northbound and southbound trains on a single track avoiding the expense of maintaining a two-track main line. The switchman visible at left is waiting for the freight train to pass. (Jay Schauer)

transported in 1991 to Anchorage distributors from producers in the Matanuska and Susitna valleys. Gravel, used mostly in construction projects, generated about $3 million, or an average of $1.50 a ton, in freight revenue. Gravel shipments by rail played a significant role in construction of the Dalton Highway, the 600-mile road that trucks travel hauling equipment and supplies to Alaska's arctic oil fields. Since Prudhoe Bay, the nation's largest oil field, was discovered, the railroad has transported equipment and supplies to Fairbanks where trucks were loaded to complete the trip to the North Slope. Though it no longer ships the large loads it did during the oil boom of the 1970s and 1980s, the railroad continues to move equipment and supplies for oil companies such as North Slope producers ARCO Alaska Inc. and BP Exploration (Alaska) Inc. In 1991, for example, the railroad shipped about 30,000 tons of pipe worth more than $1 million in freight revenue,

Locomotives are lined up at the Alaska Railroad's engine maintenance area near Ship Creek. (Diamond Arts Photography)

chemicals for oil production and other supplies.

"Maybe we missed a bet with Prudhoe," Dick Knapp, Marketing Director for the Alaska Railroad Corp., says of the railroad's decision to forego an extension to the North Slope. Yet at a cost of $1 million to $3 million a mile, laying new track is expensive. A proposal to invest $600 million to $1.8 billion for a North Slope extension in the 1970s failed to muster sufficient political or business support. Yet some Alaska officials now say hindsight shows the project had merit.

The railroad has found other ways to cash in on the oil industry's bounty. Shipments of jet fuel, gasoline, heating oil and diesel fuel made from

In 1992 the Alaska Railroad moved into its new headquarters building near Ship Creek in downtown Anchorage. The railroad leases the space from a private developer, but owns the land. (Sean Reid)

refineries in Cook Inlet and the Interior accounted for nearly $19 million or 35 percent of the railroad's 1991 freight revenue. Alaska's aviation industry and military complexes as well as consumers rely on the railroad as an important link in the transportation network that delivers petroleum products as far west as the Aleutian Islands, as far north as Norton Sound and as far south as Prince William Sound. MAPCO Alaska Petroleum and Tesoro Alaska Petroleum shipped more than 500 million gallons of petroleum products between the Interior and Anchorage by rail in 1991 at an average cost of 3.8 cents a gallon.

Tesoro sends some of its fuel products through a pipeline from its Kenai refinery to Anchorage, where it is loaded onto rail tanker cars for shipment to Fairbanks.

MAPCO Alaska, the railroad's largest customer, credits much of its growth during the past 15 years to the system's ability to efficiently move its products from its refinery at North Pole east of Fairbanks to the Port of Anchorage, which now

The Nenana depot has become a railroad museum for visitors to the Interior community at the junction of the Nenana and Tanana rivers. Tourism adds to revenues for both the Alaska Railroad and the White Pass and Yukon, and both lines have upgraded their facilities to accommodate increased tourist traffic. (Ernest Manewal)

A trailer-crane loads a Span-Alaska trailer at the Anchorage terminal. (Diamond Arts Photography)

gets 75 percent of the refiner's products. "Trucks were not economical," says A.L. "Buki" Wright, MAPCO's chief in Alaska. "We started with enough volume to contemplate building a pipeline to Anchorage, but the railroad allowed us to build our business incrementally."

The refiner currently ships 50 to 55 tank cars of fuel per day in and through Anchorage seven days a week. The demand for MAPCO's products has become so great at Anchorage International Airport that an underground fuel pipeline from the Port of Anchorage can no longer handle the volume. Now MAPCO is sending rail tanker cars directly to the airport. "The railroad has made it possible for the airport to grow," Wright says.

Petroleum products also are shipped through Anchorage to villages in western Alaska that formerly received all their fuel from the West Coast at significantly higher cost. MAPCO supplies western Alaska by sending fuel north by rail to Nenana, where it is transferred to barges for shipment on the Tanana and Yukon rivers to remote villages all the way to Norton Sound.

The railroad transports goods to and from

Canadian and Lower 48 railroads via barges operated by Crowley Maritime Services of Seattle and Canadian National Railways AquaTrain through Prince Rupert, British Columbia. Interline freight in 1991 totaled more than $10 million, or 20 percent of freight revenue. Interline freight varies from equipment and machinery to liquid natural gas, frozen fish, animal feed, automobiles, scrap metal, building supplies, newsprint, flour and staple goods. Products are shipped in rail cars from such railroads as Burlington Northern, Southern Pacific, Union Pacific and Canadian National.

The barges of Crowley Maritime Services and Canadian National Railways AquaTrain in Whittier and Sea-Land and Tote in Anchorage also bring intermodal freight, which enters or leaves Alaska in rail cars or containers. Of all intermodal freight that the railroad handles through Whittier and Anchorage, approximately 63 percent is shipped north to Fairbanks. People throughout the railbelt and even remote areas benefit from this service because groceries, beverages, electronic equipment and other consumer goods are shipped more economically by rail once they enter the state. In 1991, some 201,000 tons of intermodal shipments generated $6.5 million, or an average of $32.31 per ton, in freight revenue for the railroad.

Though the Alaska Railroad's rates are specified in published tariffs, it is difficult to compare those rates with comparable ones at other railroads. Rather, the rates are competitive with trucking and barge rates in Alaska and they vary with the distance and the commodity being shipped. Knapp says railroads have generally the same fixed costs but the more miles they are spread over, the cheaper the ton-per-mile rates. In addition, rail tariffs may be discounted for volume contracts made with large customers.

The railroad's most visible service is transporting passengers, primarily tourists. In 1991, a record 471,217 people rode the Alaska Railroad. The service includes a shuttle to Whittier for passengers and their vehicles, scenic trips to Seward, Anchorage-to-Fairbanks trips with stops at Denali National Park and winter transportation for rural residents. Though it still loses money, passenger service generated $8.1 million, or an average of $17.20 per person, in revenue in 1991. Knapp says the service is on the verge of breaking even after being promoted by the state for several years and after marketing pacts were created with major tour operators.

The Alaska Railroad is also a significant landlord with 2,300 of its 36,000 acres leased for industrial, commercial and residential uses. Revenues from ground leases and permits generate about $4 million annually. One new project is the redevelopment of the south side of Ship Creek in downtown Anchorage where the railroad has already leased a new headquarters building and co-developed the Comfort Inn. Plans call for eventual construction of a commercial complex with museums and other tourist attractions.

Using a multifaceted approach, the Alaska Railroad has become a substantial tool for economic growth and industry expansion in the state. Communities along the railbelt owe much of their development to the railroad. At least 300 out of a total of 1,200 jobs in Seward are due directly to the presence of the railroad, says Wayne Carpenter, director of the Seward Chamber of Commerce. "We've had our ups and downs...but the railroad

At Whittier and Seward, cruise ship passengers can board the Alaska Railroad for trips to Alaska's interior. Trains to Whittier, shown here with a Princess cruise ship in port, carry buses because there are no roads into the Prince William Sound port. Ship passengers board the buses and ride in style through two tunnels to join the railroad's main line at Portage on Turnagain Arm. (Jay Schauer)

is a vital part of our economy," he said.

Some say the railroad should do more to enhance economic development in Alaska by expanding its track system. However, many Alaskans have mixed feelings about the tracks pushing deeper into the wilderness.

A 1988 study by Commonwealth North, an Anchorage prodevelopment group, found that many Alaska Native village leaders were hesitant to connect with a major transportation system that would link them to the rest of the state. They feared an invasion by outsiders would exploit their wildlife, overwhelm their culture and make it impossible to control drug and alcohol abuse in the villages. "We still have images of passengers shooting buffaloes out of rail (car) windows," a Native state legislator told the study's authors. Yet Native groups recognize the potential for railroads to move their considerable natural resources to market and that the railroads might be less intrusive than highways. Increasingly, Natives are joining the campaign for some proposed extensions of the Alaska Railroad.

Proposals to extend the line have ranged from modest to farfetched. They include connecting with the Canadian rail network in British Columbia, extending the system from Nenana to the Yukon River and north to Prudhoe Bay, building a non-contiguous system from Nome to the northern Brooks Range and western Seward Peninsula, adding a leg to the proposed Nome segment that would extend to the Ambler mineral belt near Kobuk, and linking Alaska and Asia by rail with a tunnel under Bering Strait. Others call for building a rail outlet for minerals and timber

The Alaska Railroad uses this gigantic snowblower to clear their tracks in winter. (Diamond Arts Photography)

between McGrath and Bristol Bay, and in southcentral adding a feeder line from Palmer to the Sutton coal fields, extending the railroad from the Port of Anchorage to Fire Island, adding a line from Houston to Point MacKenzie, relocating the Anchorage rail yard to Eagle River and relocating the Fairbanks rail yard.

The Commonwealth North study, the most recent available, concluded that the most attractive of these extension proposals were those in which resources would be taken to market by the shortest rail route directly to deep-water ports.

Extending the railroad from Fairbanks to the Canadian border would open up East Coast markets for Alaska goods, especially frozen fish, proponents argue. Lt. Gov. Jack Coghill says Canadian officials have vowed to meet Alaska with

In this early 1980s photo, brothers Steve (left) and Chris Brown explore engine No. 556, donated to Anchorage by the Alaska Railroad in 1959, and moved by the U.S. Army to a prominent site on the downtown park strip. (Penny Rennick)

a rail system at the border, and points out that while Congress originally authorized construction of 1,000 miles of main line track in Alaska, only 483 miles have been built. "That authorization has never been rescinded, and we should cash in on that," says Coghill, who thinks the Canada extension has merit.

But opponents say that barge traffic through Whittier is the most cost effective way to move goods through Canada because it does not involve a huge capital outlay. Moreover, a 400-mile extension to the Canadian border would not provide access to significant known mineral resources in Alaska.

Yet such an extension would fit nicely with plans for the most daring of the railroad expansion proposals now being pursued. It is a plan to build an underwater tunnel across 50-mile-wide Bering

Strait to the Russian Far East. George Koumal, head of the Interhemispheric Bering Strait Tunnel & Railroad Group in Tucson, Ariz., says his organization is working to bring together varied interests in the United States, Mexico, Canada and Russia to undertake the project in the next 10 to 12 years.

Koumal says the independent group aims to link the Mexican, U.S., Canadian and Siberian rail systems at an estimated cost of $37 billion and open up access to diamond, gold, coal, oil, gas and other minerals resources on three continents as well as supporting considerable agriculture, forestry and hydroelectric potential. "The important element is for the U.S., Russian, Canadian governments to give their consent for the project," Koumal says. "We would expect a modest financial stimulus to come from the governments, but the railroad would be financed by private interests just as railroad right-of-ways were sold in the Old West."

Another proposal to gain access to northwestern Alaska's natural resources involves building a 400-mile non-contiguous rail line that would join the coal, copper and other strategic mineral deposits in that region to a future year-round deep-water port at Cape Nome or Safety. Proponents such as Arctic Slope Regional Corp. say such a system is a natural because it fits the original mission of the Alaska Railroad to link mineral deposits such as coal to markets. Even railroad officials are excited by the possibilities of bringing to market vast reserves of western arctic coal. But seasonal pack ice and lack of natural deep-water harbors near Nome must enter into any plans for this extension.

State officials are currently evaluating the possibility of building the rail line to develop the coal resource. Others note that a rail system in northwestern Alaska also could be extended 150 miles east from Selawik to Kobuk in the Ambler mineral district to tap its copper resources as well as other minerals.

Similarly, two other rail expansion plans would aid development of mineral resources in central Alaska. One calls for building a 400-mile rail line

At the Alaska West Express fuel transfer facility in Fairbanks, fuel is transferred from Alaska Railroad cars to tanks or trucks. (Jay Schauer)

BELOW:
Private tour companies contract with the Alaska Railroad to haul their domed cars along the main line from Anchorage to Fairbanks. (Diamond Arts Photography)

FACING PAGE:

The Alaska Railroad, sporting the color scheme predominant in the mid-1970s, crosses the Riley Creek trestle near Denali National Park. (Charles Kay)

along the Kuskokwim River drainage system that would connect mineral deposits and timber with a deep-water port site at Cape Newenham. The other proposal suggests adding 20 miles to the current railroad at Palmer to create a feeder line from the Sutton coal fields.

Another plan would extend the railroad 130 miles from Nenana to the Yukon River, adding six weeks to the shipping season for moving freight in and minerals and timber out of the Interior. It also would permit the use of deeper-draft barges than those now used on the Tanana River.

That extension also would open up the

possibility of another 400-mile extension to Gates of the Arctic National Park through Anaktuvuk Pass and give access to numerous mineral deposits in the northern region in addition to the opportunities for a rail link to Prudhoe Bay.

Two more extension proposals stem from notions that more efficient water transportation could be brought to southcentral Alaska by building new ports on Fire Island near Anchorage or at Point MacKenzie across Knik Arm from the city. The 40-mile extension from the main line at Wasilla to Point MacKenzie would provide access to the area's mineral deposits and give coal and timber shipments from the Interior quicker access to water transportation. When asked, railroad officials said it would cost a minimum of $50 million to lay the track for the Point MacKenzie extension. The seven-mile Fire Island extension would be built on a gravel causeway across shallow mud flats, enabling the creation of a year-round regional port on Fire Island. One study has suggested the Fire Island plan may be too costly at an estimated $1.6 billion. Alaska officials were considering both ideas in 1992.

Relocation of the Anchorage and Fairbanks rail yards also has been suggested to free up land in the downtown areas of both cities for other development.

Railroad officials say they are neutral on all of the extension proposals. However if an expansion idea is economically sound, they say the railroad will soon hear about it. Says Knapp: "When the market develops, you've got the impetus for production that stimulates the development of transportation links."

Grandview Ski Train

By Bill Sherwonit

Editor's note: *Former Outdoors columnist for the no-longer-published* Anchorage Times, *Bill has written about sled dogs and Koyukuk country for* ALASKA GEOGRAPHIC®.

Every year for more than two decades, hundreds of Anchorage-area residents have joined in a midwinter celebration: the Grandview Ski Train.

Billed as a "social event wrapped around skiing," the Grandview Train has, since 1972, primarily catered to cross-country and telemark skiers in search of pristine backcountry conditions. And an excuse to party.

Yet the origins of this Alaska institution can be traced back to the 1940s, when the ski train, now a Nordic skier's ritual, began as a downhiller's delight.

As former Alaska Railroad employee James Triber explained a few years ago, "In the '40s, '50s and early '60s, there used to be trips to Grandview once each winter, sometimes twice. But back then, it

was all downhill skiing. Nobody'd even heard of cross-country. Or very few."

Triber, who left Alaska in the early 1980s to retire in Arizona, further recalled, "Back then it was steam-run equipment. There wasn't a dance car or anything like that. But we had a baggage car where we'd sell hamburgers, hotdogs and soft drinks. And the train could be used as a warm-up lodge if people got cold skiing."

Then, as now, ski train passengers would ride the rails to Grandview, located between Portage and Seward along the rail line. Grandview is not a town, nor the site of any man-made structure. Neither is it a special geographic feature, although the name is sometimes erroneously applied to a nearby glacier.

It is, apparently, nothing more than a locale in the Chugach Mountains, and now also a spot on the map, which was once described as having a grand view. The description was appropriate: Local scenery includes rugged, knife-edged ridges,

FACING PAGE:
Skiers ready their gear beside the Grandview Ski Train, an annual Anchorage Nordic Ski Club charter of the Alaska Railroad that carries skiers south into the Chugach Mountains on the Kenai Peninsula for a day of wilderness skiing. (Bill Sherwonit)

forested valleys, glaciers and a long-distance view of Cook Inlet.

One of Grandview's prime appeals, past and present, is its isolation. No roadways or developed hiking trails lead to this spot. There are no nearby lakes or landing strips for aircraft. There is only the railroad, twisting and turning through the mountains between Anchorage and Seward.

Even the railroad is seldom used, especially in winter. No regular passenger service is scheduled. Only freight trains use the route. Grandview has an unspoiled atmosphere, and there is lots of open space, plenty to quickly swallow even 400 or 500 skiers.

Back in the train's early days, downhill skiers would travel to Tunnel Station, about six miles down the tracks. Others used a portable rope tow, provided first by the railroad and later by the local ski club.

"It didn't go very high, 100 or 200 feet," Triber said. "But you could get in a pretty good run."

The earliest train trips attracted 100 to 150 people, but by the early 1960s, numbers had more than tripled. Still, for reasons neither Triber nor anyone else seems able to remember, Grandview's downhill era ended sometime that decade.

The Grandview Ski Train took on a new life in 1972, in a reincarnated form that was certainly bigger than its earlier version.

One of the trip's reorganizers, John Baxandall of Anchorage, says the Nordic Ski Club charged $5 for adults and $15 for families. To make the package even more attractive, Baxandall invited the Anchorage Krausenspieler Blaskapelle German Band to entertain the crowd.

Expecting only 200 to 300 people, the club sold all its tickets in less than half an hour.

The reincarnated ski train's first trip took place March 19, 1972, and by all accounts was a success. Not surprisingly, word quickly spread and more than 1,000 people signed up for the 1973 train.

Interest continued to grow through the mid- and late 1970s, finally peaking in the mid-1980s, when the Anchorage Nordic Ski Club, which annually organizes the trips, ran as many as four ski trains per winter. Enthusiasm waned late in the decade, but began to revive in the early 1990s.

The Krausenspieler band, which specializes in polkas, has remained a prime attraction. For more than two hours on the return trip to Anchorage, the band plays music while railroad revelers sway, bump and jump to the music.

Bibliography

Clifford, Howard. *Doing The White Pass*. Seattle: Sourdough Enterprises, 1983.

Cohen, Stan. *Rails Across The Tundra*. Missoula, Mont.: Pictorial Histories Publishing Co., 1984.

Fitch, Edward M. *The Alaska Railroad*. New York: Frederick A. Praeger, Inc., Publishers, 1967.

Janson, Lone E. *The Copper Spike*. Anchorage: Alaska Northwest Publishing Co., 1975.

Minter, Roy. *The White Pass*. Fairbanks: University of Alaska Press, 1987.

Prince, Bernadine LeMay. *The Alaska Railroad In Pictures 1914-1964*. Vols. 1 and 2. Anchorage: Ken Wray's Print Shop, 1964.

Wilson, William H. *Railroad in the Clouds: The Alaska Railroad in the Age of Steam, 1914-1945*. Boulder, Colo.: Pruett Publishing Co., 1977.

Index

ALASKA GEOGRAPHIC. back issues

The North Slope, Vol. 1, No. 1. Charter issue. Out of print.

One Man's Wilderness, Vol. 1, No. 2. Out of print.

Admiralty...Island in Contention, Vol. 1, No. 3. $7.50.

Fisheries of the North Pacific, Vol. 1, No. 4. Out of print.

The Alaska-Yukon Wild Flowers Guide, Vol. 2, No. 1.
Out of print.

Richard Harrington's Yukon, Vol. 2, No. 2. Out of print.

Prince William Sound, Vol. 2, No. 3. Out of print.

Yakutat: The Turbulent Crescent, Vol. 2, No. 4. Out of print.

Glacier Bay: Old Ice, New Land, Vol. 3, No. 1. Out of print.

The Land: Eye of the Storm, Vol. 3, No. 2. Out of print.

Richard Harrington's Antarctic, Vol. 3, No. 3. $12.95.

The Silver Years, Vol. 3, No. 4. $17.95.

Alaska's Volcanoes: Northern Link In the Ring of Fire,
Vol. 4, No. 1. Out of print.

The Brooks Range, Vol. 4, No. 2. Out of print.

Kodiak: Island of Change, Vol. 4, No. 3. Out of print.

Wilderness Proposals, Vol. 4, No. 4. Out of print.

Cook Inlet Country, Vol. 5, No. 1. Out of print.

Southeast: Alaska's Panhandle, Vol. 5, No. 2. Out of print.

Bristol Bay Basin, Vol. 5, No. 3. Out of print.

Alaska Whales and Whaling, Vol. 5, No. 4. $19.95.

Yukon-Kuskokwim Delta, Vol. 6, No. 1. Out of print.

Aurora Borealis, Vol. 6, No. 2. $14.95.

Alaska's Native People, Vol. 6, No. 3. $24.95.

The Stikine River, Vol. 6, No. 4. $12.95.

Alaska's Great Interior, Vol. 7, No. 1. $17.95.

A Photographic Geography of Alaska, Vol. 7, No. 2. $17.95.

The Aleutians, Vol. 7, No. 3. $19.95.

Klondike Lost, Vol. 7, No. 4. Out of print.

Wrangell-Saint Elias, Vol. 8, No. 1. $19.95.

Alaska Mammals, Vol. 8, No. 2. $15.95.

The Kotzebue Basin, Vol. 8, No. 3. $15.95.

Alaska National Interest Lands, Vol. 8, No. 4. $17.95.

Alaska's Glaciers, Vol. 9, No. 1. Out of print.

Sitka and Its Ocean/Island World, Vol. 9, No. 2. $19.95.

Islands of the Seals: The Pribilofs, Vol. 9, No. 3. $12.95.

Alaska's Oil/Gas & Minerals Industry, Vol. 9, No. 4. $15.95.

Adventure Roads North, Vol. 10, No. 1. $17.95.

Anchorage and the Cook Inlet Basin, Vol. 10, No. 2. $17.95.

Alaska's Salmon Fisheries, Vol. 10, No. 3. $15.95.

Up the Koyukuk, Vol. 10, No. 4. $17.95.

Nome: City of the Golden Beaches, Vol. 11, No. 1. $14.95.

Alaska's Farms and Gardens, Vol. 11, No. 2. $15.95.

Chilkat River Valley, Vol. 11, No. 3. $15.95.

Alaska Steam, Vol. 11, No. 4. $14.95.

Northwest Territories, Vol. 12, No. 1. $17.95.

Alaska's Forest Resources, Vol. 12, No. 2. $16.95.

Alaska Native Arts and Crafts, Vol. 12, No. 3. $17.95.

Our Arctic Year, Vol. 12, No. 4. $15.95.

Where Mountains Meet the Sea: Alaska's Gulf Coast,
Vol. 13, No. 1. $17.95.

Backcountry Alaska, Vol. 13, No. 2. $17.95.

British Columbia's Coast, Vol. 13, No. 3. $17.95.

Lake Clark/Lake Iliamna Country, Vol. 13, No. 4.
Out of print.

Dogs of the North, Vol. 14, No. 1. $17.95.

South/Southeast Alaska, Vol. 14, No. 2. Out of print.

Alaska's Seward Peninsula, Vol. 14, No. 3. $15.95.

The Upper Yukon Basin, Vol. 14, No. 4. $17.95.

Glacier Bay: Icy Wilderness, Vol. 15, No. 1. Out of print.

Dawson City, Vol. 15, No. 2. $15.95.

Denali, Vol. 15, No. 3. $16.95.

The Kuskokwim River, Vol. 15, No. 4. $17.95.

Katmai Country, Vol. 16, No. 1. $17.95.

North Slope Now, Vol. 16, No. 2. $14.95.

The Tanana Basin, Vol. 16, No. 3. $17.95.

The Copper Trail, Vol. 16, No. 4. $17.95.

The Nushagak Basin, Vol. 17, No. 1. $17.95.

Juneau, Vol. 17, No. 2. $17.95.

The Middle Yukon River, Vol. 17, No. 3. $17.95.

The Lower Yukon River, Vol. 17, No. 4. $17.95.

Alaska's Weather, Vol. 18, No. 1. $17.95.

Alaska's Volcanoes, Vol. 18, No. 2. $17.95.

Admiralty Island: Fortress of the Bears, Vol. 18, No. 3. $17.95.

Unalaska/Dutch Harbor, Vol. 18, No. 4. $17.95.

Skagway: A Legacy of Gold, Vol. 19, No. 1. $18.95.

ALASKA: The Great Land, Vol. 19, No. 2. $18.95.

Kodiak, Vol. 19, No. 3. $18.95.

ALL PRICES SUBJECT TO CHANGE.

Your $39 membership in The Alaska Geographic Society includes four subsequent issues of *ALASKA GEOGRAPHIC*®, the Society's official quarterly. Please add $10 for non-U.S. memberships.

Additional membership information is available upon request. Single copies of the *ALASKA GEOGRAPHIC*® back issues are also available. When ordering, please make payments in U.S. funds and add $2.00 postage/handling per copy book rate; $4.00 per copy for Priority mail. Non-U.S. postage extra. Free catalog available. To order back issues send your check or money order and volumes desired to:

The Alaska Geographic Society

P.O. Box 93370
Anchorage, AK 99509

NEXT ISSUE: *Prince William Sound*, Vol. 20, No. 1. From a watery wilderness loaded with fishing and recreational opportunities to a major oil industry terminal, Prince William Sound delicately balances environmental values with prodevelopment economics. This issue will look at the region's resources; its economic hub at Valdez; its Native people, the Chugach Eskimos; and the spectacular surroundings that make the Sound one of Alaska's most popular recreation spots. To members 1993, with index. $18.95.

AUSTIN POST: Alaska's Ice Maven...see page 92

ALASKA'S COAL

By L. J. Campbell

In several regions of the state, millions of dollars are being quietly spent exploring and trying to develop Alaska's coal reserves.

Coal played a strategic part in the history and early development of Alaska. Today, only one commercial coal mine operates in the state, producing about 1.5 million tons a year for domestic and export markets. However, economists predict a growing demand for coal through the next two decades, particularly in Asian and European countries where more coal will be needed to fuel electrical power generators. This need, say coal developers, opens opportunities for Alaska to snag perhaps as much as 10 percent of the increase in the world market. In turn, this could stimulate commercial production of Alaska coal, creating jobs and bringing some revenue to the state, which gets royalties and taxes from coal sales and some rental income from coal land leases.

"A lot of people are doing a lot of work to make Alaska an exporter of coal within the next 10 years, at the outside," said Dick Swainbank, minerals specialist with the Alaska Department of Commerce and Economic Development.

The state has nearly 1.8 billion tons of measured or proven coal reserves, according to R.B. Stiles,

president of the Alaska Coal Association and general manager of the Diamond Shamrock/Chuitna Coal Joint Venture project in the Beluga coal field. Various state and federal estimates put the state's coal resources at between around 5.5 trillion tons, about a third of the nation's total coal supply. This hypothetical resource figure is based on the possibility of coal occurring in given geological structures. The bulk of Alaska's coal resources are thought to be in the Northern Alaska Coal Province.

While the resources estimate means little in practical terms, it indicates Alaska's tremendous potential for vast holdings of high quality coal, says Gary D. Stricker with the U.S. Geological Survey, Branch of Coal Geology in Denver. "If industry or government had the money to pursue resource evaluation to drill holes, those billions of reserves would increase quite dramatically into the trillions," Stricker said. "There are great areas in Alaska about which no information is known, but we're totally convinced there is coal."

Alaska's coal types include anthracite, the highest ranking, most burnable coal, as well as the

Subbituminous coal from Usibelli Coal Mine near Healy is loaded aboard a coal ship bound for Korea from the Port of Seward. (Steve McCutcheon)

second highest ranking coal, bituminous. Subbituminous coal, the only type now being commercially mined in Alaska, is a wetter coal often used in combination with higher ranking coals. The big selling point for Alaska's coal is its low sulfur content, an attractive feature in this environmentally sensitive age when sulfur emissions from coal-fired generators are linked to acid rain, air pollution and possibly global warming.

Yet, development of Alaska's coal reserves — most of which are located in remote regions — is thwarted by high exploration costs and a lack of transporation and markets.

Exploration costs in Alaska are about three times those in the Lower 48, making Alaska coal development a higher risk investment. The direct mining costs are about the same in Alaska as for mines elsewhere, although capital requirements are greater since a larger inventory of parts and supplies are needed.

A big drawback to coal development is the lack of roads, rails, ports and loading facilities. Building such a network in remote

These facilities at the Port of Seward handle coal destined for the Korea Electric Power Corp. (Harry M. Walker)

regions can double the cost of a project. The only coal loading facility in the state is located at the Port of Seward, at the southern terminus of the Alaska Railroad about 358 miles from Usibelli Coal Mine and about 150 miles from the Matanuska coal field. Some potential coal developers on that route say that for Alaska coal to compete in the Pacific Rim export market, transportation costs need to drop $4 to $5 a ton, either through government subsidies or by shortening the haul to tidewater, which would mean building a new port in upper Cook Inlet.

Currently, the only domestic market for coal is in the Interior, where five power generating plants burn coal produced at Usibelli Coal Mine. Other domestic users may come on line, but are still several years off. A new 53-megawatt power plant planned for the mid-1990s under the federal Clean Coal Technology program could take additional coal from Usibelli. For the past decade, various state and private studies have looked at using coal to generate electricity for north-western Alaska, arctic communities and the Red Dog lead/zinc mine, all of which are now served by diesel and oil. The Arctic Slope Regional Corp. has stepped up its efforts to develop in-state and export markets for bituminous coal from its western arctic lands.

Currently, the export market for Alaska coal is limited to the

Republic of Korea; the Korea Electric Power Corp. (KEPCO) buys about half of Usibelli's annual output, marketed by Suneel Alaska Corp. A sluggish world market for coal, with supply exceeding demand, has caused coal prices to drop. In 1992, Usibelli and its partners — the Alaska Railroad Corp. and Suneel — made price concessions to match the world benchmark price set by Australian-Japanese contracts, to entice KEPCO to extend its contract.

The world market situation is pre-dicted to change in about 1995 with increasing demand from European and Asian countries, primarily Taiwan, Japan and Korea. This increased demand—an additional 100 million to 200 million tons through about the year 2010—may present the market Alaska coal needs to attract investors. This coal is bought in incremental increases through futures contracts being traded now. At least two large projects—Idemitsu Alaska Inc. in the Matanuska coal field and Diamond Chuitna in the Beluga coal field—are aiming at that export market.

A mammoth knot hangs in the way of marketing Alaska coal, however, and this is the tangled Mental Health Lands Trust now in litigation (see box, page 86). A court injunction has frozen a million acres originally in the trust, and this injunction affects virtually all coal fields in the state that were part of the original trust lands. The Diamond Chuitna project, for instance, is located on 20,000 acres of state lands — all original mental

health trust lands — and Stiles says coal cannot be marketed until access is assured and royalties established through some kind of settlement. Currently the state collects 5 percent in coal royalties off its land, but the mental health trust might not be limited to this amount. The uncertainty about royalties complicates estimating production costs and determining a selling price.

Here is a chronological look at the history of Alaska coal:

1786 Capt. Nathaniel Portlock, an English trader, finds coal on the Kenai Peninsula at Coal Cove, now Port Graham, near Seldovia.

1849 Peter Doroshin, a graduate of the Imperial Mining School at St. Petersburg, investigates Alaska's mineral resources. During his four-year reconnaissance, he visits many coal outcroppings along the Pacific Coast.

1855 Upon Doroshin's recommendation, the Russian American Co. opens a coal mine at Port Graham. Alaska's first coal mine uses American-made equipment and German miners to produce 30 to 35 tons a day. The coal is intended for export to San Francisco, but loses the market to higher rank coal from Vancouver Island. It is used instead for local and maritime markets until 1865.

1862 First coal is mined in Southeast, from Sepphagen Mine on Admiralty Island, and supplies USS *Saginaw* with fuel in 1869.

1879 Whaling ships and U.S. revenue cutters start using coal from a mine near Cape Sabine along the arctic coast.

1881 Capt. C.L. Hooper takes on 20 tons of coal for the *Corwin* at the mine near Cape Sabine and names it the Corwin Mine after his ship.

1888 The Wharf Mine opens near Port Graham, to supply lignite and subbituminous coal on a commercial basis at between 1,000 and 3,000 tons a year, for between $3 and $6 a ton.

Coal from the Thetis Mine on the arctic coast supplies the U.S. Revenue cutter *Thetis*.

1893 Alaska Mining and Development Co. opens a small coal mine near Chignik Lagoon; Alaska Packers Association opens the Chignik River Mine that supplies coal to a local fish cannery and steamships until 1911.

1895 An appropriation from Congress allows the U.S. Geological Survey to assess Alaska's mineral resources for the first time. Dr. W.H. Dall studies coastal coal deposits.

1897 The Alaska Commercial Co. opens a mine on the Nation River near Eagle and takes out about 2,000 tons of coal for steamboat boilers.

1898 The Beluga-Yentna coal fields are noted.

Yukon sternwheelers use coal as fuel to transport gold seekers to gold fields. At least 16 mines operate along the Yukon River until about 1910, when river traffic decreases to mostly boats using oil fuel. The Pickhart brothers open a mine on the south bank of the Yukon, 10 miles above Nulato, later taken over by Alaska Commercial Co.; several hundred tons of coal are mined for riverboat use before it is abandoned in 1902. The Alaska Commerical Co. also mines about 900 tons of coal from a site on the lower Yukon River, about 125 miles from Nulato. The Blatchford Mine about nine miles below Nulato produces 300 tons of coal.

Coal is also used to thaw frozen ground for placer mining, and at least 100 small mines operate around the turn of the century.

1899 Eleven companies have filed for railroad routes, envisioning access to Alaska's Bering River coal field a guarantee of success.

1900 U.S. mining laws are extended to the Territory of Alaska, allowing prospectors to stake coal claims on government-surveyed land. Numerous claims are staked in Bering River and Matanuska Valley coal fields by prospectors apparently unaware that there were no government-surveyed lands in any Alaska coal fields.

The Cook Inlet Coal Fields Co., headed by Homer Pennock, builds the town of Homer and mines rich coal seams near Bluff Point, west of the present town. A railroad is built to the end of Homer Spit. Several companies previously mined scant coal beds east of the spit, in short-lived attempts that ceased by 1897.

More than 1,000 tons of coal are taken from the Corwin Mine and shipped to Nome. Small-scale mining by Alaska Development Co., Arctic Development Co. and the Corwin Trading Co. extract coal from Corwin Mine for shipboard use.

Coal is reported on Nunivak and Nelson islands and a few tons are mined for local use.

1902 Yukon River steamers begin converting coal and wood burners to petroleum-fueled engines.

The Williams Mine on the east bank of the Yukon, about 90 miles below Nulato, opens with a 400-foot shaft. About 1,700 tons of coal are produced in the first year.

1903 George C. Martin maps the Bering River coal field for the U.S. Geological Survey.

Construction of the Alaska Northern Railway from Seward revives prospecting for coal in the Matanuska Valley. The Chicago Creek Mine, near Candle on the Seward Peninsula, taps into an 80-foot lignite seam and produces almost continuously until 1940, despite early attempts by the federal government to halt the mine's unlicensed exploitation. The coal is used by placer gold miners.

A 40-foot tunnel opens the Bush Mine, on the south bank of the

The Evan Jones Coal Mine, which opened in 1920 in the Matanuska Valley, produced coal for the military bases in Anchorage until the late 1960s when the bases converted to natural gas. (Steve McCutcheon)

The Healy Clean Coal Project, shown in this artist's drawing, would operate as a federal demonstration plant for clean coal technology during its first year of power production, projected for 1996. The project was awaiting its final state permit from the Alaska Department of Environmental Conservation in late 1992. The federal Environmental Impact Statement was expected to be available by winter 1992-1993, and project developers hope to begin construction in 1993. The Alaska Industrial Development and Export Authority will own and operate the plant after its year as a federal pilot project. The plant will use about 300,000 tons of coal a year — a combination of run-of-mine and waste coal — from Usibelli.
(Courtesy of Usibelli Coal Mine, Inc.)

Yukon four miles below Nulato; about 400 tons of coal is taken for steamboat use.

1904   The Alaska Coal Act eliminates the requirement that coal claims be on government-surveyed land and most previous claims are relocated. About 900 claims are filed under this Act, but because of apparent fraudulent claims of a few "corporations" all claims become suspect. Spurred by articles in the *Washington Press* newspaper and *Collier's Weekly* magazine, Alaska coal claims become a national issue that fuels the growing ideological feud between Gifford Pinchot, Chief of the Bureau of Forestry and 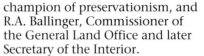 champion of preservationism, and R.A. Ballinger, Commissioner of the General Land Office and later Secretary of the Interior.

A.J. Collier conducts a geological reconnaissance south of Cape Beaufort.

1905   George Martin maps the Matanuska coal field.

1906   President Theodore Roosevelt closes Alaska public lands to entry for coal as a result of controversy over Alaska coal claims.

1907   Roosevelt creates the Chugach National Forest, which includes coal claims in the Bering River fields.

1908   Congress validates Roosevelt's withdrawal of Alaska public lands.

Capt. Theielen opens a mine on the Kobuk River about a mile below Kallarichuk River.

The Alaska Peninsula Mining and Trading Co. operates the Hook Bay Mine in the Chignik field.

1910   Andrew Kennedy with the General Land Office and G. Wingate for the Forest bureau study coal properties in the Bering River field. The two men disagree about the commercial quantities of coal; Calvin A. Fisher, of the U.S. Geological Survey, is sent to analyze the area.

Testimony before Congress reveals that some General Land Office staff have been on a Bureau of Forestry payroll, hired apparently to disrupt and delay land office patenting operations and to leak information to Pinchot with which to embarrass Ballinger. In the meantime, Alaska coal claimants are required to continue annual assessments, but cannot mine or sell coal. Most coal claims are abandoned. The railroads planned to access the Bering River coal fields are never built.

At this time, only 2 percent of the coal consumed in Alaska is produced in the territory; most is imported from Washington, British Columbia, Australia and Japan at an average price to consumers of $15 a ton. Local coal would have cost about $3 a ton.

1911   Federal coal laws prompt uprisings in two Alaska towns close to the Bering River fields where local coal remains untouched and claimants and investors suffer financial ruin. Angry Cordovans host the "Cordova Coal Party" and dump several tons of imported coal into Prince William Sound, after luring the federal marshal out of town with reports of a fictitious shooting. According to Sen. Ernest Gruening at the time: "On May 4, 1911, the following cable was sent to the Associated Press from Cordova: 'The excitement caused by the Government's failure to hurry action on the Alaska land cases reached a climax here today, when 300 businessmen and citizens formed in a body and, armed with shovels, marched to the ocean wharf of the Alaska Steamship Company, where they proceeded to throw several hundred tons of British Columbia coal into the bay....Chief of Police Dooley ordered the crowd to disperse, but President Adams, of the Chamber of Commerce, shouted: 'Shovel away, boys. We want only Alaskan coal.'"

Pinchot is burned in effigy at Katalla, the budding port of entry to the Bering River coal fields, then a town of several thousand people.

1913   U.S. Navy investigates the Bering River field, taking 1,100 tons of its reportedly high quality coal for shipboard testing. The samples contain much slate and gravel and are considered unsuitable for steamer coal; Bering River coal receives a bad reputation.

1914   Total reported coal production in the territory reaches 47,969 tons, valued at about $362,000, while coal imports have reached more than 1.5 million tons. Most of the domestic production comes from the Wharf Mine at Port Graham, but includes several thousand tons of coal from the McDonald Property on Bering Lake in 1907. Not included is the pirated output of the Chicago Creek mine, or mines at Herendeen Bay, Chignik Bay and Unga Island, operated in conjunction with local canneries.

Congress passes Alaska Coal Leasing Act allowing commercial development of Alaska coal mines, resulting in mines in the Nenana, Matanuska Valley and Bering River coal fields and what will become Mount McKinley National Park.

Passage of the Alaska Railroad Act authorizes purchase of the abandoned Alaska Northern Railway and construction of the Alaska Railroad. President Woodrow

Wilson chooses a route to Fairbanks that passes the Matanuska, Little Susitna, Broad Pass and Healy coal fields. This creates the market and transportation necessary for large scale mining.

The U.S. Navy tests coal from the Matanuska field, finding it suitable for naval use. The Alaska Engineering Commssion and the Navy's Alaskan Coal Commission spend the next eight years prospecting and mining to supply the railroad and Navy ships in the Pacific with coal.

1916   The Alaska Railroad reaches Matanuska coal field near Palmer.

1917   In January, the first long-term successful coal mining venture opens in the Matanuska field at the Eska Mine. Coal is sledded three miles to Sutton at a rate of 35 tons a day until the Eska Creek rail spur is finished. An Anchorage Chamber of Commerce bulletin reports two coal companies operating in the Matanuska field with a daily output of 200 tons. "These coal fields are the government's hobby and promise great future development from which Anchorage will receive the major benefit," the bulletin says.

1918   The Alaska Railroad reaches Nenana coal field near Healy. The first commercial coal mine in this field opens four miles east at Suntrana by the Healy River Coal Corp., headed by Austin "Cap" Lathrop. Horse-drawn sleds transport the coal to Healy for use by the railroad.

1919   On June 10, 110 tons of coal from the Chickaloon Mine in the Matanuska field are loaded aboard the U.S. Navy gunboat *Vicksburg* at Anchorage.

1920   The Evan Jones Mine opens in the Matanuska field.

The Bering River Coal Co. opens tunnels in the Carbon Creek area.

1921   A coal washing plant is constructed by the Alaska Engineering Commission, in charge of building the railroad, and the Navy Alaskan Coal Commission. The Navy commission completes a base camp with housing, school and hospital at Chickaloon.

1922   A 4.4-mile railroad spur from Healy to Suntrana Mine is completed.

Usibelli Coal Mine extracts subbituminous coal from seams such as these in the Hoseanna Creek Valley. (Chris Arend, courtesy of Usibelli Coal Mine, Inc.)

1923   The Alaska Railroad reaches Fairbanks.

The Mount McKinley Bituminous Coal Co. opens the Yanert Mine, within Mount McKinley National Park.

1924   Privately operated mines furnish coal needed by the railroad and new communities. Government mines at Eska and Chickaloon in the Matanuska Valley are closed. No coal is ever loaded onto Navy ships; before the mines and handling facilities are fully developed, the Navy converts

Mental Health Lands Trust

In 1956 the federal government selected a million acres in the Territory of Alaska as a land trust to pay for mental health programs, since at the time all mentally ill were sent out of the territory for treatment. Most of Alaska's major coal deposits were included in these selections. The state legislature abolished the trust in 1978 and assigned the trust lands the same status as other state lands. In 1982, the Alaska Mental Health Association sued the state. The Alaska Supreme Court ordered in 1985 that the trust be reestablished with original lands. The next five years were spent unsuccessfully trying to reach a compromise settlement. The matter ended up back in the courts, with an injunction blocking transfer of lands originally in the trust and raising questions about the validity of the title on lands already transferred.

Of the original lands, about 45,000 acres have been conveyed to individuals; 40,000 to Native corporations; 40,000 to municipalities; 54,500 are in coal leases; 132,000 are in oil and gas leases; 62,000 are in mining claims; and 372,000 are in state parks, refuges and forests.

its coal-burning ships to oil.

1925 The Premier Mine opens in the Matanuska field and operates until 1982. The Hecky, or Coal Creek, Mine opens and operates until 1930.

1926 Fairbanks Exploration Co. builds a coal-fired plant in Fairbanks to power its gold dredges and contracts with the Suntrana Mine for coal.

1928 The Harkrader Mine opens on Admiralty Island and ships coal to Juneau, but closes a year later due to financial problems.

1929 Alexander Haralan renews mining on the Kobuk River, at a site opened in 1908, for use in placer mining.

1935 Emil Usibelli comes to Alaska to work in the Matanuska coal field at the Evan Jones Mine.

1937 An explosion in the Evan Jones Mine kills 14 men and shuts down production.

1938 Emil Usibelli starts a logging operation in Suntrana to supply timbers for the underground mines.

1940 Coal production reaches 174,000 tons a year, with production in the territory from 1880 to 1940 totalling 2,612,629 tons, most of which is bituminous coal from the Evan Jones Mine in the Wishbone Hill district of the Matanuska coal field and subbituminous coal from Healy

River and Suntrana mines of the Nenana coal field. The Healy River Mine is the largest, yielding more than half the coal produced in Alaska. Its largest customer is the U.S. Smelting, Refining and Mining Co., which uses the coal to power its dredges and large placer mining operations near Fairbanks.

1941 Alaska Railroad reopens Eska Mine in the Matanuska field to supply new military bases in the Anchorage area. The military buildup in Anchorage and Fairbanks during and after World War II creates incentive for further exploration and development, and additional mines are opened at Healy, Nenana, Jarvis Creek, Broad Pass, Costello Creek and in the Little Susitna and Wishbone Hill areas of the Matanuska Valley. The price of coal jumps 50 percent. Lack of fuel forces mines to open in Wainwright and Barrow.

1943 Emil Usibelli and partner T.E. Sanford obtain a U.S. Army mining license and open a surface coal mine east of Suntrana. The company contracts with the Army to supply newly constructed Ladd Field (now Fort Wainwright) with coal.

1946 Alaska Railroad begins replacing coal-burning engines with diesel locomotives and closes its Eska Mine in Matanuska Valley.

1948 Emil Usibelli purchases his partner's share and the Usibelli Coal Mine (UCM) is incorporated in the Territory of Alaska.

1950 Cap Lathrop, principal owner of the Healy River Coal Corp., dies in a mine accident at Suntrana.

Total coal production in the territory reaches 412,000 tons for the year.

1951 The Fairbanks Municipal Utilities System builds a coal-fired power plant.

1952 A coal-fired power plant is constructed at Eielson Air Force Base near North Pole. Lathrop's Healy River Coal Corp. is sold to the Suntrana Mining Co. to settle inheritance taxes.

1954 The conversion of railroad locomotives from coal to diesel fuel is complete. The changeover does not adversely affect the Alaska coal industry because of growth in the military market. Production doubles to a peak of 865,000 tons a year.

Alaska Commissioner of Mines Phil Holdsworth suggests the Beluga coal field could be the source of mine-mouth power for Anchorage area.

Morgan Coal Co. explores on the Kukpowruk River with a 70-foot tunnel.

1956 American Exploration & Mining Co. (later Placer Amex Inc. and now Placer Dome U.S. Inc.) acquires the Evan Jones Coal Mine.

1957 Natural gas is discovered in the Cook Inlet basin.

1959 Alaska becomes the 49th state. The U.S. Bureau of Mines drills for coal near Beluga Lake.

1961 UCM purchases the Suntrana Mining Co. A 21-megawatt coal-fired power plant is built at Clear Air Force Station in Anderson.

Union Carbide investigates the Kukpowruk River coal.

1962 UCM closes underground mining operations at Suntrana.

1963 Vitro Minerals Mine, a venture of R&P Coal and Vitro Minerals, opens east of Suntrana.

1964 Emil Usibelli is killed in a mining accident and his 25-year-old son Joe takes over as company president. The University of Alaska Fairbanks constructs a coal-fired power plant.

1966 American Exploration & Mining Co. (Placer Dome) applies for its first coal prospecting permits in the Beluga area.

Coal production increases, reaching about 925,000 tons a year.

1967 Fort Richardson and Elmendorf Air Force bases convert coal-fired steam power plants to natural gas from Cook Inlet. Matanuska mines, except for Premier, close after losing these major military markets. Golden Valley Electric Association opens a 25-megawatt mine-mouth power plant at Healy.

1969 Congress enacts the Mine Safety and Health Act.

1970 UCM purchases the Vitro Minerals Mine and becomes the only remaining commercial coal mine operating in Alaska.

Kaiser Engineers begin a seven-year mining and economic evaluation of western arctic coal.

1971 UCM begins its land reclamation program and forms a subsidiary, Nuera Reclamation. The UAF coal-fired power plant in Fairbanks is expanded.

1973 OPEC oil embargo and a severe winter result in oil and gas shortages and an increased interest in and demand for other energy sources, including coal. UCM signs its first long-term contract to supply coal to military bases.

1977 President Jimmy Carter's energy policy includes conversion of utilities and industry to coal, prompting renewed interest in Alaska coal. Congress passes the Surface Mining Control and Reclamation Act. UCM sells Nuera Reclamation.

Mobil Oil Co. applies for leases on 23,000 acres in the Yentna River basin.

1978 UCM leases land from the Alaska Railroad and develops the Tri-Valley subdivision to provide modern housing for mine employees.

1979 Placer Dome studies a mine-mouth coal-fired electric power generation plant in the Beluga field.

1980 Resource Associates of Alaska, a subsidiary of NERCO

Minerals Co., explores the Chignik field for the Bristol Bay Native Corp.

1981 The Korean Alaska Development Co. conducts exploratory drilling in the Bering River field for Chugach Alaska Corp.

Diamond Shamrock-Chuitna Coal Joint Venture (DSCCJV) starts a multiyear $25 million to $40 million exploration and development effort in the Beluga field.

1982 UCM establishes a regulatory compliance department to deal with increasingly complex and numerous permitting requirements laws and regulations. The state raises royalty and rental rates for state coal leases.

Placer Dome and Cook Inlet Region Inc. obtain $4 million grant from the U.S. Department of Energy

The MV Vigan docks at the coal port at Seward to take on coal shipped by Suneel Alaska Corp. on the Alaska Railroad from Healy. (Steve McCutcheon)

to do coal gassification feasibility study. Placer and two Japanese companies — Electric Power Development Co. and Nissho Iwai Corp. — do $2.5 million study of truck/conveyor transportation from Beluga field to a new port.

DSCCJV ships a 250-ton bulk sample to Japan and a 150-ton bulk sample to the Lower 48 for utilization testing.

1983 With the Alaska Surface Mining Control and Reclamation Act, the state assumes regulatory authority from the federal government for permitting all coal mining in Alaska.

Placer Dome starts three-year study of minimal tonnage mining out of Beluga field using existing dock facilities near Tyonek.

The state explores the Cape Beaufort-Kukpowruk River coal areas.

1984　In July, UCM signs a 15-year contract with Suneel Shipping Co. to export coal to Korea Electric Power Corp. for fueling a converted oil-fired electric power generation plant in Honam, Korea.

Construction of the Seward Coal Terminal is completed.

1985　First shipment of Usibelli coal leaves for Korea in January. To satisfy increased production for the Korea coal export contract, UCM's work force is increased 42 percent with the addition of 36 employees.

Hawley Resources Group Inc. drills for the Alaska Division of Geological and Geophysical Surveys at Chicago Creek as part of state studies to provide coal for electrical power generating plants at Kotzebue and other northwestern Alaska communities.

DSCCJV files the first permit application for a new mine under the Alaska Surface Coal Mining Control and Reclamation Act.

1987　UCM ships coal to Taiwan for testing by the Taiwan Power Corp. and to Japan for testing by the Electric Power Development Corp.

1989　In August, the Alaska Industrial Development and Export Authority, Golden Valley Electric Association, UCM and engineering and technology companies submit an application to the U.S. Department of Energy for funding a 53-megawatt power plant at Healy under the federal Clean Coal Technology program. In December, the Energy Department selects the project for matching federal funding of up to $93.2 million. Also in December, coal sales total 207,540 tons, a UCM monthly record.

1990　The Alaska Legislature appropriates $25 million from the Railbelt Energy Fund for the Healy Clean Coal Project. UCM supplies six Interior Alaska power plants with a total of 790,000 tons of coal while an additional 797,000 tons are shipped through the Port of Seward to the Republic of Korea.

1991　In April, the U.S. Congress approves the Healy Clean Coal Project. In June, UCM sets a fiscal-year production record of more than 1.6 million tons. In September UCM receives a five-year renewal of its Poker Flats surface mining permit near Healy.

1992　In September, the Alaska Public Utilities Commission okays the sales agreement for Golden Valley Electric Association to buy power from Healy Clean Coal Project.

Idemitsu Alaska Inc.'s plans to develop a coal mine at Wishbone Hill in the Matanuska coal field remain on hold pending settlement of Alaska's Mental Health Lands Trust litigation.　■

ALASKA COAL DEVELOPMENT UPDATE
Current Mines / Projects

■ USIBELLI COAL MINE, INC.

The only commercial coal mine operating in Alaska. Located near Healy, in the Nenana Province. Produces about 1.5 million tons a year of subbituminous coal with average 0.17 percent sulfur content. Leases 18,000 acres from the state with 150 to 200 million tons identified reserves. Employs 110 to 120. Sells to Golden Valley Electric Association; Clear Air Force Station; Fairbanks Municipal Utility System; Fort Wainwright Army Base; Eielson Air Force Base; University of Alaska Fairbanks; Reliable Coal Co.; and Suneel Alaska Corp., which exports about half the mine's annual production to the Korea Electric Power Corp.

■ ATQASUK MINE

This small subbituminous mine is located on the Meade River about a mile from the village of Atqasuk, 80 miles south of Barrow, in the Northern Alaska Province. Since about 1987, the mine has operated two to three weeks a year to produce 300 tons of coal. The stockpiled coal is delivered to Atqasuk in the winter to heat about 30 homes equipped with coal stoves. The mine is operated by Arctic Slope Consulting Group, Inc., a subsidiary of Arctic Slope Regional Corp. and is part of the Western Arctic Coal Demonstration Project sponsored by the North Slope Borough. Discussions ongoing about building a small coal-burning power plant to generate electricity and heat water for village use.

■ DEADFALL SYNCLINE

Located in the western part of Northern Alaska Province, project of Arctic Slope Regional Corp. (ASRC), 40 miles south of Point Lay, 70 miles north of Red Dog lead/zinc mine and just west of the National Petroleum Reserve-Alaska boundary on ASRC land. Resources of bituminous, ultra-low sulfur coal in the western Arctic estimated at 3 billion tons. Deadfall Syncline reserves undisclosed. Small mine six miles from coast has been producing about 500 tons a year since 1986 to supply coal for home heating in Point Lay, Point

Hope and Wainwright as part of North Slope Borough's Western Arctic Coal Demonstration Project. In 1992, 1,000 tons produced, of which 380 tons were distributed to villages in the project and 500 tons were earmarked for test shipment to Japan. Arctic Slope Consulting Group Inc. is in charge of development and marketing. Geologist and project manager Teresa Imm said a 500,000-ton-a-year contract is needed to begin commercial production. Various state and ASCGI studies associated with mine development include: transportation alternatives; coal-fired generating plants at Nome, Red Dog, Kotzebue, Adak, the Pribilofs; beluga whale migration surveys; mine reclamation; sea ice movements. Attempts are underway to get federal funds for Arctic Mining Research and Development Program to study effects of permafrost on large-scale mining.

■ WISHBONE HILL

Project of Idemitsu Alaska Inc., subsidiary of Idemitsu Kosan Co. Ltd. Located between Palmer and Sutton in Matanuska field. Exploration and development initiated in 1983. Originally set to began production 1992, but full permitting not obtained until September 1991 because of mental

health trust lands litigation. Project on hold until mental health trust issue settled. Expenditure to date more than $9 million with development and replacement capital estimated at $60 million. Production from surface mining estimated to be 750,000 to 1 million tons of bituminous coal a year for 15 to 20 years; employment at 200. A $10 million project to widen 12 miles of the Glenn Highway, to accommodate coal truck traffic, started summer 1992 with state/federal/Idemitsu money.

■ HOBBS INDUSTRIES INC.

Castle Mountain and Evan Jones projects: Both projects, located in the Matanuska coal field, originally intended to supply U.S. Air Force backscatter radar station to be built at Glennallen. Surface mining at Castle Mountain fully permitted, but development halted by mental health lands litigation. Evan Jones underground mine properties then subleased from Placer Dome U.S. Inc. Permitting to reopen mine still in progress when Air Force scuttled its backscatter project. Randy Hobbs, president of Hobbs Industries, said his company is maintaining permits on both properties and looking for other markets. Investment so far about $2 million.

■ DIAMOND CHUITNA

Located in Beluga coal field on 20,000 acres of state leases, all original mental health trust lands. Project is 80 percent permitted but on hold pending lands trust settlement. Plans are to surface mine 330 million tons of subbituminous coal, haul by truck to a new deep-draft port at Ladd on Cook Inlet for shipment primarily to Asian markets. Project investment to date, $40 million to $50 million. Project owners are Starkey Wilson, Richard Bass, William Hunt and Diamond Shamrock/ Chuitna Coal Joint Venture. DSCCJV, composed of two subsidiaries of Maxus Corp., is in charge of development and marketing.

■ BELUGA COAL CO.

Located in Beluga coal field. Beluga Coal Co. is jointly owned by Placer Dome and Cook Inlet Region Inc. Resources estimated at 1 billion tons of subbituminous coal with 500 million tons mineable reserves. Placer has been doing exploratory drilling in the area since first obtaining prospecting permits beginning in 1967. Coal is located near tidewater; potential customers are power utility companies on the U.S. West Coast, Hawaii, Mexico, Japan, Korea and Taiwan

ALASKA'S COAL RESOURCES AND RESERVES

PROVINCE-BASIN-FIELD	HYPOTHETICAL RESOURCES[1] (MILLIONS OF TONS)	IDENTIFIED / MEASURED RESOURCES[1] (MILLIONS OF TONS)	MEASURED RESERVES[2] (MILLIONS OF TONS)	COAL RANK*	DOMINANT MINERAL OWNERS[3]	CURRENT ACTIVITY
■ **NORTHERN ALASKA COAL PROVINCE**						
Western Arctic Coal Fields:						
Wainwright Area				S	Arctic Slope Regional Corp.	
Kukpowruk Area	1,200	275 / 20		B	Arctic Slope Regional Corp.	
Cape Beaufort Area	1,700	390 / 45		B	Arctic Slope Regional Corp.	
Deadfall Syncline Area	5,000	500 / 60		B	Arctic Slope Regional Corp.	Deadfall Syncline Project
Lisburne Area				B to A	Arctic Slp. Reg. Corp./U.S. Govt.	
All Other Areas	3,992,100	148,835 /		S & L	U.S. Govt.[4]/State of Alaska	Limited Local Use
Province Totals	**4,000,000**	**150,000 / 125**				
■ **COOK INLET-SUSITNA PROVINCE**						
Broad Pass Field	500	50 /		L & S	State of Alaska	
SUSITNA BASIN:						
Susitna Field	2,300	110 /		S	State of Alaska	
Yentna Field	2,500	1,000 /	500	S	State of Alaska	
COOK INLET BASIN:						
Matanuska Field	500	150 /	45	B to A	State of Alaska/ Mental Health Trust	Idemitsu Alaska Inc. Hobbs Industries
Beluga Field:	30,000	10,000 /	1,000			
Capps District				L to S	Cook Inlet Region Inc.	Beluga Coal Co.
Chuitna District				S	State of Alaska/ Mental HealthTrust	Diamond Chuitna Project Center Mine Project Lone Ridge Mine Project
Threemile District				S	State of Alaska/ Mental Health Trust	Beluga Coal Co.
Kenai Field:						
Onshore	35,000	320 /		S	State of Alaska	
Offshore	1,500,000		N/A	S & B	State of Alaska	
Province Totals	**1,570,800**	**11,630 /**	**1,545**			
■ **NENANA PROVINCE**						
NENANA BASIN:						
Hosanna Creek Field	7,000	4,900 /	250	S	State of Alaska/Mental Health	Usibelli Coal Mine
Healy Creek Field	2,000	1,000 /		S	State of Alaska	
Western Nenana Field	450	300 /		S	U.S. Dept. Int./NPS	
Tatlanika Creek Field	400	290 /		S	State of Alaska	
Wood River Field	350	275 /		S	State of Alaska	
Jarvis Creek Field	175	75 /		S	U.S. Dept. Int./BLM	
Rex Creek Field	130	70 /		S	State of Alaska	
Mystic Creek Field	100	55 /		S	State of Alaska	
West Delta Field	50	20 /		S	State of Alaska	
East Delta Field	25	15 /		S	State of Alaska	
MINCHUMINA BASIN:						
Little Tonzona Field	3,000	1,500 /		S	U.S. Govt./State of Alaska	
Other Nenana Province Deposits	1,000	100 /		S to B		
Province Totals	**14,680**	**8,600 /**	**250**			

PROVINCE-BASIN-FIELD	HYPOTHETICAL RESOURCES[1] (MILLIONS OF TONS)	IDENTIFIED / MEASURED RESOURCES[1] (MILLIONS OF TONS)	MEASURED RESERVES[2] (MILLIONS OF TONS)	COAL RANK*	DOMINANT MINERAL OWNERS[3]	CURRENT ACTIVITY
■ ALASKA PENINSULA PROVINCE						
Chignik Field	1,500	230 /		B	Bristol Bay Native Corp.	
Herendeen Bay Field	1,500	130 /		B to L	The Aleut Corp./U.S. Govt.	
Other Alaska Peninsula Deposits	150	70 /		L to B		
Province Totals	**3,150**	**430 /**				
■ GULF OF ALASKA PROVINCE						
Bering River Field	3,500	110 /		B to A	Chugach Alaska Corp.	
Other Gulf of Alaska Deposits	500			B		
Province Totals	**4,000**	**110 /**				
■ YUKON-KOYUKUK PROVINCE						
UPPER KOYUKUK BASIN:					U.S. Dept. Int./BLM, F&WS	
Tramway Bar Field	75	15 /		B	U.S. Dept. Int./BLM	
LOWER KOYUKUK BASIN:					Doyon Ltd. & U.S. Dept. Int.	
Nulato Field	50			B	Doyon Ltd.	
KOBUK BASIN:					U.S. Govt. & NANA Reg. Corp.	
Kobuk Field	10			B	NANA Regional Corp.	
Other Yukon-Koyukuk Deposits	1,000			B		
Province Totals	**1,135**	**15 /**				
■ UPPER YUKON PROVINCE						
Eagle Field	100	10 /		S & L	Doyon Ltd. & U.S. Dept. Int.	
Rampart Field	50			S & L	Doyon Ltd. & U.S. Dept. Int.	
Other Upper Yukon Deposits	1,000			S & L		
Province Totals	**1,150**	**10 /**				
■ SEWARD PENINSULA PROVINCE						
Chicago Creek Field	10	5 /		L & S	NANA Regional Corp.	
Other Seward Peninsula Deposits	100			L & S		
Province Totals	**110**	**5 /**				
■ OTHER COAL BEARING AREAS						
Copper River Field				L	State of Alaska	
Admiralty Island				B	U.S. Dept. Agriculture/FS	
Yukon-Kuskokwim Region				S	Calista Corp/U.S. Dept. Int.	
ALASKA TOTALS	**5,595,025**	**170,800 / 125**	**1,795**	**L to A**		

[1] Values for Hypothetical and Identified Resources taken from Special Report 37, Alaska Dept. Natural Resources, Division of Mining and Division of Geological and Geophysical Surveys, except Northern Alaska Coal Province resources, which were taken from Alaska's High-Rank Coals, Information Circular 33, August 1990, Alaska Division of Geological and Geophysical Surveys.

[2] Measured Reserves are from various documents available to the general public and 1992 verbal communications with various development entities.

[3] Dominant Mineral Owner based on area owned as shown on Dept. of Interior, Bureau of Land Management, ALASKA, Land Status Map, June 1987.

[4] U.S. Govt. implies one or more agencies within the Dept. of Interior, i.e. Bureau of Land Management (BLM), U.S. Fish and Wildlife Service (F&WS), National Park Service (NPS), and Forest Service (FS).

* L = Lignite, S= Subbituminous, B= Bituminous, A= Anthracite   **Chart courtesy of R.B. Stiles, D&R Ventures, Inc., adapted by _ALASKA GEOGRAPHIC_®.**

Ice Maven

By Richard P. Emanuel

The next time you see an aerial photograph of an Alaska glacier, check the photo credit. There is a fair chance that it will read "Austin Post." Post retired from the U.S. Geological Survey 10 years ago, but at 70, he still spends part of each summer prizing secrets from Alaska's rivers of ice. His primary target for the last four years has been Bering Glacier, North America's longest and largest glacier. Bering Glacier has begun a catastrophic retreat that, if scientists are right, will reveal in coming decades a network of fiords some 60 miles long, rivaling Glacier Bay.

The theory upon which glaciologists base their prediction of Bering Glacier's retreat was advanced by Post 20 years ago with respect to Columbia Glacier. Post's insights into the workings of tidewater glaciers, which terminate in the sea, are probably his chief theoretical contribution to the study of glaciers. Equally vital have been his photographic catalog of North America's glaciers and his observations of surging glaciers, particularly in Alaska.

In an age when doctorates are the union cards of many disciplines, Post, whose flowing gray hair and beard evoke the image of Walt Whitman, exemplifies what the uninitiated but gifted individual can offer. "I got into glaciology through the back door," he happily states. "I never got a college education. Didn't particularly want one."

Austin Post grew up in the apple orchards around Lake Chelan, Wash., on the eastern slope of the Cascade Mountains. "Getting up into those mountains was what I wanted to do," he recalls. He set his sites on joining the U.S. Forest Service. With a friend, he built his own fire lookout station when he was 14. "We built two," he says. "Wind got the first one." His office today is graced with a faded photo of the second wooden tower.

When Post turned 16, he landed a job as a real fire lookout for the Forest Service. "I got my dream station, Pyramid, [the loftiest in that part of the Cascades], just before the war." During World War II, he was a ship's carpenter in the Navy. That led, in 1949, to a stint on a U.S. Coast and Geodetic Survey ship, mapping the seafloor in Prince William Sound. It was Post's first Alaska adventure.

With the Forest Service again after the war, Post met Lawrence Nielsen, a research chemist who was studying glacial ice flow because it resembles the behavior of certain plastics. Post accompanied Nielsen on hikes to Cascades glaciers and assisted him in his field work. The connection led to work on the Juneau Icefield and then to McCall

ABOVE: *Ten years into retirement, Austin Post, 70, still spends part of each summer conducting field work on Alaska glaciers. When not in the field, Post lives with his wife on Vashon Island in Washington's Puget Sound. (Richard P. Emanuel)*

RIGHT: *In 1899, distinguished geologist Grove Karl Gilbert of the U.S. Geological Survey first studied Columbia Glacier as a member of the Harriman Alaska Expedition. To document how the glacier had changed since Gilbert's day, Austin Post relocated one of the points from which Gilbert had viewed and photographed the glacier, but the site was so overgrown it was impossible to see the ice except from a treetop vantage point. In August 1989, 90 years after Gilbert's first glimpse of Columbia Glacier, Post shimmied up this tree for a modern look. (Dennis Trabant, USGS)*

Glacier, in what is now the Arctic National Wildlife Refuge.

Post's work on McCall Glacier began during the International Geophysical Year, 1957-1958. His job was to keep weather instruments running. In his free time, he studied aerial photographs of other Brooks Range glaciers, mapping and plotting them on topographic maps. When he spotted a notice in a glaciology journal inviting research proposals, he got an idea: "Maybe I can get paid to do this."

Post had previously purchased three war-surplus aerial cameras for $60 apiece. He had had nothing particular in mind when he bought them. Now he proposed to use them to compile a photographic record of glaciers in northwestern North America. Starting in 1960, the National Science Foundation funded a four-year photographic survey, administered by the University of Washington. Post grabbed his cameras and flew to Alaska where he hired bush pilot Don Sheldon to fly the Alaska and Aleutian ranges from Talkeetna to Port Heiden. Then the pair turned eastward and flew the ice-clad

During more than 20 years, Austin Post took tens of thousands of aerial photographs cataloging glaciers in Alaska and northwestern North America. Here, Kachemak Glacier, which drains into Bradley Lake and Kachemak Bay, descends from Harding Icefield in a photograph was taken in August 1964. (Austin Post, USGS)

coastal mountains to Ketchikan. "We followed a clear patch between storms all the way," Post recalls. "Every time we stopped for gas, we had to hurry to catch up. It was a remarkable trip." After the 1964 earthquake, to document quake effects Post rephotographed Alaska glaciers for Mark Meier of the U.S. Geological Survey. Meier recognized Post's gifts and kept him on staff in Tacoma, Wash., where he tapped him for many research efforts.

Among other things, until he retired in 1982, Post continued to annually photograph many glaciers.

Post's aerial catalog of snow and ice started at a good time. In 1960, a number of Alaska glaciers were undergoing or had recently finished what are now called surges. Glaciers typically flow a few feet a day but some have been known to briefly reach speeds 100 times faster. In the Alaska Range northwest of Paxson, Black Rapids Glacier was nicknamed the Galloping Glacier after it advanced three miles during the winter of 1936-1937, cruising as much as 115 feet a day. Such feats were considered oddities until Post began to peruse his photographs.

Glaciers erode and accumulate along their base and sides a mass of rocky debris called a moraine. When ice streams merge, the debris at their sides joins into a medial moraine, which looks like a highway dividing line. When a glacier in a side valley surges, a bulging loop forms in the medial moraine, which then looks like a dividing line painted by a drunken crew.

Post saw in some glaciers rhythmic loops of medial moraine. Surges repeat at regular intervals, he concluded: They are cyclic events. In his photographs, he identified more than 120 surging glaciers in Alaska, plus about half that number elsewhere in North America. They are geographically grouped. They occur in the Alaska Range, the Saint Elias Mountains near Yakutat and Glacier Bay, the eastern Wrangell Mountains and easternmost Chugach Mountains. They seem absent from the Coast Mountains of southeastern Alaska and the Kenai and Chugach mountains of Prince William Sound.

Why do surging glaciers occur where they do? Twenty years after Post raised that question, he concedes, "To be truthful, we still do not know." Glacial surges occur in glaciers both large and small, in wet and dry climates, at varying elevations, in temperate and subpolar settings. Theory and field observations implicate an internal cause: the collapse of the glacier's plumbing and the resulting buildup of water beneath the ice. But why one glacier surges and another does not remains mysterious.

In the mid-1970s, as the Valdez oil terminal was built, glaciologists became concerned with iceberg production in Prince William Sound. Post spent parts of two years outfitting a 40-foot ex-Navy boat, the *Growler*, so he could map the seafloor in front of tidewater glaciers. Surveys soon revealed shoals of glacial moraine near the terminus of Columbia Glacier. There were remnants of similar shoals in other fiords. It was Post who first saw the implications.

In a stable tidewater glacier, icebergs calve at a rate that is balanced by ice flowing to the terminus. The glacier erodes and deepens its bed as it builds a shoal by dumping debris from its front. Columbia Glacier, the largest in Prince William Sound, was stable prior to 1979. Part of its four-mile-wide terminus was grounded on Heather Island, the rest lay on a shallow moraine shoal. But long-term ice-loss, perhaps from global warming, led the glacier to pull off Heather Island and retreat from its self-made shoal. The glacier now ends in deeper water, icebergs calve faster and the glacier is in retreat. Columbia Glacier could recede 25 miles during the next 50 years. Bering Glacier, east of the Copper River, is even larger than Columbia

In another of Post's aerial photographs, valley glaciers descend from the Grewingk-Yalik glacier complex (upper right), south of Harding Icefield and visible from Homer across Kachemak Bay. Nuka Glacier drains to the left, and Battle Creek Glacier flows downhill at lower right. (Austin Post, USGS)

and it too may have begun a catastrophic retreat. Both glaciers may uncover stunning new fiords. Shoals near the mouths of existing Alaska fiords suggest that all this has happened before.

Austin Post lives with his wife, Roberta, in a house he built on Vashon Island, in Puget Sound. He has come far for a kid who wanted to get into the mountains he could see from his backyard lookout. With little formal education, he has relied on an active mind, hands and curiosity. "He's just a natural," says Will Harrison, a University of Alaska Fairbanks glaciologist. Bruce Molnia, director of the USGS Bering Glacier study, says Post's lack of schooling may have had advantages. His ideas about the rapid retreat of tidewater glaciers sprang not from an analysis of arcane ice physics but from clear insight into an essentially mechanical process.

And that is fine with Post. "I'm not a mathematician," he proclaims. "I'd a lot sooner fly around in an airplane, myself." As for his deeper motivation? Post is clear on that, too. "The things are pretty," he says of glaciers. "I like to look at 'em. What are the things up to?"

AERIAL PHOTOGRAPHS AVAILABLE

From 1960 through his retirement in 1982, Austin Post took 80,000 to 100,000 aerial photographs of glaciers throughout Alaska and elsewhere in western North America, as well as a series in Greenland. All of Post's North American aerial photographs are available through a public archive maintained by the U.S. Geological Survey in Tacoma, Wash. For more information, contact David R. Hirst, U.S. Geological Survey, Ice and Climate Project, University of Puget Sound, Tacoma, WA 98416, or telephone (206) 593-6516.

Musk Oxen Expanding Their Range

As the helicopter flew low over the valley, wildlife biologist Randi Jandt carefully scanned the ground for the animal some Eskimos call *Oomingmak*, "animal with skin like a beard." Blending in with ground vegetation and rock outcroppings, the *Ovibos moschatus* was difficult to spot.

"We counted heads for the census last winter," Jandt said, "because the dark coats are easier to see against the white snow." So this July, she and other Bureau of Land Management scientists flew to the Seward Peninsula to identify vegetation types at eight areas where they had seen musk oxen during the winter.

Biologists think that the selection of an overwintering area is no coincidence. There must be preferred food and possibly shelter that attracts the musk oxen back to the same area year after year. "Biologists believe that a bachelor bull will spend up to nine years in a new wintering area before cows and calves join him," Jandt said.

Increasing numbers of musk oxen on public lands on the Seward Peninsula are forcing state and federal land managers to realize just how little they know about the habits and needs of these unusual creatures. Land managers want to learn enough about musk oxen to enable them

Almost 700 musk oxen inhabit the Seward Peninsula, where populations of the animals have been growing by about 15 to 20 percent a year. (George Wuerthner)

to choose land use options that will not degrade musk ox habitat.

A total of 61 musk oxen were transplanted to the Seward Peninsula in 1970 and 1981, and their numbers have been increasing about 15 to 20 percent a year. In 1992, a joint census by BLM, the Alaska Department of Fish and Game and the National Park Service found almost 700 musk oxen in several small herds. The musk oxen have been off-limits to hunters, and with

continued protection, their numbers should increase.

"Even more significant than their increased population is their expansion into new locations, a long way from where they were first introduced," Jandt said. "For continuation of the species, we want them to have a wide geographic distribution. If there is a devastating event, such as disease, drought or a winter with severe icing in one area, the musk oxen in another area may not be affected."

Jandt says little is known about the habitat requirements of musk oxen on the peninsula, but selection of winter habitat is critical. In other places where they have been studied, such as the North Slope, Nunivak Island and Greenland, areas with shallow or windblown snow are important in the winter. Musk oxen do not move around a lot in winter, since their short legs and compact bodies are not well-adapted for traveling through deep snow.

"They may not move around much in summer, either," said Brian Bogaczyk, BLM botanist. "When we checked eight known wintering areas this July we saw a few herds within a few miles of where they spent the winter." Biologists have observed that musk oxen seem to be able to satisfy their needs for food, water and protection from predators and weather within a much smaller geographic area than the far-ranging caribou, or even moose.

—BLM-Alaska

The Great Bear, Contemporary Writings on the Grizzly, edited by John Murray, Alaska Northwest Books, Seattle, Wash. 248 pages, two maps, softcover, $14.95.

Unlike the gut and gore bear books that sensationalize maulings and glorify hunts, *The Great Bear* offers meditations on the past, present and future of grizzlies in a world of diminishing wilderness.

With a cover bearing names of the country's foremost nature writers such as Edward Abbey, Aldo Leopold, Adolph Murie, John McPhee and Frank Craighead, *The Great Bear* begs to be opened and devoured. The 17 selections include writings from Alaskans John Haines, Rick McIntyre and Richard Nelson. Readers will not be disappointed. The prose is clear, lively and eloquent, and the authors are well informed on the natural history of the grizzly.

The writers approach their common topic with great diversity. Adolph Murie draws from his years observing the bears of Denali National Park for his narrative "The Ways of Grizzly Bears," which opens the book. Writer and poet John Haines describes surprising a bear while hiking to a hunting cabin in the Tanana River region, having to shoot it in self-defense, and his vision of meeting it later, angry and wounded. Doug Peacock, an outspoken defender of grizzlies and the character model for George Hayduke of Edward Abbey's *Monkey-Wrench Gang*, tells about a grueling trip into deep grizzly country of the Continental Divide in northern Montana. He links his recovery from the Vietnam War, where he served as a Green Beret, to his pursuit of the grizzly. And National Park Service ranger Rick McIntyre, in "Grizzly Cub," from his 1990 book by the same name, replays the last troubled days of a garbage-addicted bear named Stony, a poignant example of what can happen when, even with the best intentions, man tries to manage the wild.

Several of the writers suggest that something vital is missing without the existence of wildness, represented so completely by the grizzly bear; even if we never see it, or experience it other than knowing it is there.

The book's epilogue identifies three themes that persist throughout: communion, liberation and renewal. The bear as a sacred animal is rooted in ancient cultures and is particularly evident in cultural anthropologist Richard Nelson's piece, an except from his treatise on the Athabaskan Indians of the Koyukuk River, *Make Prayers to the Raven*. To these Alaska Natives, the bear is so powerful that men may not speak of him, nor women look at him. The liberation theme presents the bear as a symbol of political freedom. The third theme, renewal, comes through celebrating nature, its regenerative powers and wildness.

Editor John Murray, an English professor at the University of Alaska Fairbanks and author of numerous nature books, chose the best of modern writings about this powerful creature, "so that grizzly lovers everywhere might find their favorite authors in one convenient volume." He provides a short introduction to each writer, along with the original source of the essays that appear in *The Great Bear*.

Murray grouped the essays by geographic regions corresponding to grizzly habitats — Alaska, the Northern Rockies, Yellowstone National Park, the Southwest. In addition, he includes maps showing where the authors are located, areas in which grizzlies are known or thought to exist, and areas slated for possible grizzly bear restoration.

Grizzlies have been considered a "threatened" species in the Lower 48 since 1973, and today occupy only 1 percent of their original habitat below the Canadian border. Of the 6,000 grizzlies estimated to live today on the North American continent, about 5,000 of them are in Alaska.

Murray's anthology is a book with a purpose: To advocate for the grizzly at a time when protection of bear habitat and development of bear management policies are subject to increasing political and commercial pressures. All royalties from the book go to the Nature Conservancy's programs for acquiring and preserving grizzly habitat.

As bear biologist Frank Craighead writes: "Alive, the grizzly is a symbol of freedom and understanding — a sign that man can learn to conserve what is left of the earth. Extinct, it will be another fading testimony to things man should have learned more about but was too preoccupied with himself to notice."

—*L.J. Campbell*

STATEMENT OF OWNERSHIP, MANAGEMENT & CIRCULATION

ALASKA GEOGRAPHIC® is a quarterly publication, home office at P.O. Box 93370, Anchorage, AK 99509. Editor is Penny Rennick. Publisher and owner is The Alaska Geographic Society, a non-profit Alaska organization, P.O. Box 93370, Anchorage, AK 99509. *ALASKA GEOGRAPHIC®* has a membership of 6,692.

Total number of copies	18,476
Paid and/or requested circulation	
Sales through dealers, etc.	1,102
Mail subscription	6,692
Total paid and/or requested	
circulation	7,794
Free distribution	210
Total distribution	8,004
Copies not distributed	
(office use, returns, etc.)	10,472
TOTAL	18,476

I certify that the statement above is correct and complete.

—Kevin J. Kerns
Business Manager

Published by
THE ALASKA GEOGRAPHIC SOCIETY

Penny Rennick,
EDITOR

Kathy Doogan,
PRODUCTION DIRECTOR

L.J. Campbell,
STAFF WRITER

Jan Westfall,
MARKETING MANAGER

Kevin Kerns,
BUSINESS & CIRCULATION MANAGER

© 1992 by The Alaska Geographic Society